Play or Be Played

What Every Female Should Know About Men, Dating, and Relationships

Tariq "K-Flex" Nasheed

A FIRESIDE BOOK
Published by Simon & Schuster
New York   London   Toronto   Sydney

FIRESIDE
Rockefeller Center
1230 Avenue of the Americas
New York, NY 10020

FIRESIDE and colophon are registered trademarks
of Simon & Schuster, Inc.

Designed by Christine Weathersbee

Manufactured in the United States of America

10   9   8   7   6   5   4   3

Library of Congress Cataloging-in-Publication Data Is Available

ISBN 0-7432-4492-3

For information regarding special discounts for bulk purchases,
please contact Simon & Schuster Special Sales at 1-800-456-6798
or business@simonandschuster.com

To Taria M. Nasheed

Contents

Introduction

It's Saturday night, and me and my peeps are hanging out at one of our regular Hollywood nightclub spots. The scene is typical of a Saturday night. Lots of dime piece females and ballin' brothas in the place. Me and my partners are checkin' out the ladies and doing our thing as usual.

This night in particular, I've made some very interesting observations. Most of the very attractive women are just standing around, trying to act extra cute. And most of the guys are basically ignoring them. No one is mingling with these women at all.

I just happen to see a lady friend of mine that I have known for years, named Stacey. Now Stacey doesn't look half as good as the other women in the club. At first glance, you wouldn't think Stacey was that attractive at all. To be totally honest, Stacey sort of looks like a wet donkey with a weave. But the amazing thing about her is that she has almost every man in that club sweating her, and she's not dressed hella hoochie either.

Stacey had men buying her drinks back to back. She had

different men stepping to her asking her to dance. She even had other *women* trying to buy her drinks and dance with her.

So why did Stacey, who is average looking on a good day, have all those men in the club giving her so much attention, while the other, more attractive females were basically being ignored?

It's because Stacey had *game.*

Other more attractive females in the club were *trying* too hard to present themselves in the best light. These women were *trying* to look sophisticated. These women were *trying* to appear interesting. These women were *trying* to *act* confident.

Stacey didn't try to be anything. She just *was.*

Stacey *was* confident. Stacey *was* sophisticated. And Stacey *was* interesting.

Many women will go to a social spot, and purposely act *anti*-social. Which completely defeats the purpose of going to a social setting. But Stacey understood the basic, simple premise of going to a social place. She was there for the same reasons the men were there. She wanted to *socialize.*

Stacey's attitude showed that she was totally comfortable with herself, and this is what attracted people to her. Stacey had a very bubbly, fun, and positive attitude whenever she went out, and this attitude compensated for her physical shortcomings.

Like I said, I've known Stacey for years, and she is one of the coolest people you would ever want to meet. Whenever I see her out at the clubs, she always offers to give me one of her drinks. In fact, so many guys buy her drinks, she can't carry all the glasses at the same time.

Her very sexy attitude and confident demeanor make people comfortable whenever they are around her. Stacey knows how to get guys to come out of the pockets for her too. She has always had guys buying her gifts, paying for her trips. I mean this girl's game is impeccable. Every major city I travel to, I'm likely to run into Stacey, because she has had some guy fly her into town.

While other, more attractive women are sitting around, broke, relying on their looks to get them over, women like Stacey know how to rely solely on their game. By the time you finish with *Play or Be Played,* you are going to know what women like Stacey know. And even though you might not want to use your knowledge to get guys to buy you gifts or take you on trips, you will be able to use this knowledge and game any way you please.

A few years ago, Stacey was just another insecure female with a lot of self-esteem issues and self-doubt, who constantly made bad choices in men. Then one day, she decided to let go of the "I'm-a-strong-sista-and-I-don't-need-help" façade, and she stepped to me and asked me to put her up on game. I did, and it changed her life. And with this book, I'm going to lace you with the same game I gave Stacy.

Now I know many of you ladies hate the term "game." The first thing many women think of when they hear the word game is conning someone, deceiving someone, or doing something scandalous. And many women will say things like "I hate game," and "I don't want to be part of no games."

The reality is this. Having game, or not having game, can not only affect your relationship choices, it can affect every aspect of your life.

How Game Affects Every Aspect of Your Life

We live in a society based on capitalism. The basic theory behind capitalism is people using and manipulating others for their own benefit. And capitalism affects *every* aspect of our lives. There will always be people trying to contribute to you or trying to con you. So it is imperative that you have game so you can peep where people are coming from.

The word game, in street terms, simply means intelligence, hustle, and common sense. And having game means being knowledgeable about every endeavor you choose to engage in. If you don't have game, in *every* aspect of your life, there will be people who will simply try to get over on you. Again, since we live in a society founded on capitalism, this theory applies to every aspect of your life. For instance, if you are seeking a new job, and the employer sees that you don't have any game about yourself, he might try to use that to his advantage. And that employer might have you working extra hours without giving you adequate pay.

Ladies, how many times have you been at the mall trying on an outfit that you *knew* didn't look good, and the sales clerk was still like "girl, that's you." That sales person will have you walking around looking like a hoochie Power Ranger, because you have no game.

Ironically, many women do have game in their lives *except* when it comes to dating. These women know how to get out there and hustle for the best jobs, the best education, the best deals at the mall, or the best medical plans. But when it comes to dating, many women choose to shut down all forms of logic, and just wish and hope for the best.

Now ladies, before you can successfully administer game, you have to be de-programmed, and re-programmed. You have to be debriefed of all the misinformation that has been given to you. One problem is that certain sectors of society have encouraged a head-in-the-sand mentality that many women have toward dating.

Play or Be Played is a self-help guide for females who want to know the real deal about dating, and how men *really* think.

This book will teach women how to screen guys, and what signs to look for in order to not get played.

What is unique about this book is that it is coming from the experiences of a former player and self-admitted mack. Sure, there are other relationship books geared toward women, but the information you'll find in those books is usually second-hand, and compiled from the experiences of people other than the author.

Play or Be Played comes straight from the horse's mouth. As a former hustler and player, it was my job to study women, and learn what made them tick. In the process, I learned a lot about myself and basic human behavior, especially when it came to interacting with the opposite sex. I learned how men and women tend to put their best foot forward in the beginning stages of relationships, and the only way to see beyond the façade they present is to have some level of game.

When my book *The Art of Mackin'* became a best-seller, the primary audience for the book was men. But when I began appearing on all the television talk shows, and going on radio shows around the country, more women started buying the book than guys. To this day, I get thousands of letters and e-mails from women asking for my expertise on relationships, because many women have never heard a man break the game down like this before. A lot of women were asking me to write a version of *The Art of Mackin'* for them, and this is why I wrote *Play or Be Played*.

Now this isn't another one of those books by male authors who are trying to gain brownie points from women by bashing other men. I'm going to let women see themselves through the unfiltered view of real men. Some of the language and philosophies in this book may seem somewhat harsh at times, but I would be doing women a disservice to sugarcoat the truth. So

I'm going to discuss the dating game the way real men discuss women and dating when women aren't around.

It has become popular to tell women they are victims, and that everything negative that happens in a woman's life is some man's fault. This mindset has become very detrimental in the so-called "movement" to empower women. By playing the role of a victim, people can waive responsibility for the consequences of their actions and choices. This book will help women understand how to avoid the victim role and how to make better choices when it comes to dealing with men.

Teaching women how to choose the *right* mate is really half the battle. When the average man realizes that he is not dating the *right* female, or the female he thought she was, he will sever the relationship or simply move on to another female. But women will remain in denial and keep on dating a man they *know* isn't worth a damn. When the relationship goes sour, I refuse to accept the argument that he wasn't like that in the beginning. Visiting rooms at jails and prisons have so many girlfriends, wives, and baby mamas there on visiting day, you would think they are shooting a music video. But women justify staying in these dysfunctional relationships by claiming they were taught to be loyal, and to stand by their man no matter what. This is a bunch of BS. *Play or Be Played* will explain the *real* reasoning behind this behavior.

Play or Be Played will be a self-help guide for women, showing them how to identify some of the reasons why they have made so many poor dating decisions.

By reading this book, women will learn the real deal about key dating issues, such as:

1. What all men want.

2. How to tell if a guy is a potential cheater.

3. The best way to *keep* a man once you get him.

4. How to spot a scrub.

5. How to tell if a man is *only* interested in sex from you.

6. What it takes to get with a baller.

Play or Be Played will give women an opportunity to be honest with themselves and identify and rectify certain negative qualities they may possess. Many women aren't getting the dating results they desire because they are engaging in hoochie or chickenhead behavior. And the sad thing is these women don't even realize they exhibit this behavior. So I have compiled a Chickenhead Test on p. 75, so women can see where they stand on this issue.

Relationship books, especially for black women, like to approach the subject from a spiritual point of view. Well, it's time out for that. When you have real relationship issues, you need real solutions to those issues. If you are a woman who has invested a lot of time in a relationship with a brotha who is basically bullshitting you around, all that "Find a way to center yourself," and "Channel the energy of your inner child," New Age mumbo jumbo isn't going to help you in the long run.

I'm not going to break this game down like a New Age guru.

I'm gonna break it down like an old-school mack.

I often hear women who have been in a number of dysfunctional or failed relationships say things like "I have terrible luck with men." It's not that these women have bad *luck*. They have bad *strategies* when it comes to dealing with men. Luck is something you can't control. That's where you waive responsibility and leave everything up to chance. But you can control your strategies when looking for a potential mate, and sitting around wishing and hoping for Mr. Right isn't going to do the trick. You have to acquire some game and dating techniques so you can make your chances of finding Mr. Right more of a reality.

So ladies, if you want a brotha to tell you what you want to hear, so that you can feel good temporarily, I suggest you put *Play or Be Played* down, and go pick up a Brian McKnight CD. But if you are tired of the BS and you finally want to know the real deal, you've come to the right place.

Now I know many of you ladies might ask, "Tariq, what are *your* credentials? How are you qualified to tell women about themselves? How are you able to give women advice on dating and relationships?"

Well ladies, I'm qualified to tell you about the dating game, because I have lived the player lifestyle. I have lived the mack lifestyle. And most of the knowledge I have acquired over the years I learned from older professional street players and hustlers.

I have found that the same principles that apply to man-woman relationships on a street level apply to man-woman relationships in the square (or mainstream) world. And for the first time, ladies, you get to see the intricacies of man-woman relationships and the dating game from a mack's point of view.

Basically this book is offering you the truth. Many people are afraid to be completely honest with females, because often-times, the truth can be risky and offensive.

With this book, I'm willing to take that risk. If you're not afraid of the truth, turn the page.

1: What Men Really Want

I was appearing as a guest on this one talk show, discussing my philosophies on relationships, and one of the topics was "How a women can please her man." There were a couple of female authors on the panel who were trying to explain what men want, and how a woman can make them happy, and so on. These women were so off the mark, it was ridiculous.

They were advising women to use all sorts of sex toys, scented powders, exotic oils, and bubble baths. One of the women on the panel actually advised women to use a dildo on their man if they want to get him aroused.

These women were so caught up in relaying their misinformation they didn't even bother to notice the uncomfortable reactions coming from the men in the audience. As I looked around, I saw some of the male audience members cringing as they listened to the nonsense coming from these female "experts." These women were going on about how women can please their men by using candles, rose petals, aroma beads, and the like, until I just broke in and said what was on all the fellas' minds.

"Look ladies, men don't really like none of that stuff. We're relatively simple. If you want to please us, just give us oral sex and food."

The men in the audience erupted into applause. The women on the panel were flabbergasted. One of the female panelists replied, "Well, some men like these sexual accessories." I explained to her that men will *tolerate* those accessories, because they don't want to do anything to kill the mood. But generally, men can do without all those foreplay items.

Then, one of the ladies made the million-dollar statement that revealed their real agenda.

"Well, what about a woman's needs?"

But the topic was supposed to be about how women can please their man. You see, that's the problem. A lot of women claim they want to know how to please their man, but they really have an ulterior motive.

Ladies, men are very, very simple. If women aren't pleasing their men, it is because they *don't want* to please their men. If a woman has an Indian-giver mentality, or if she is disingenuous in her motives, men who may be looking at her as a potential mate can sense that.

Many women ask me what it takes to keep a quality man. Yet, when I then ask them, "If you want a *quality* man, what are you *willing* and able to bring to the table?" a lot of these women are stumped. At the same time, many of these women have a whole list of "what I ain't gonna do" for a man.

The four most common items on the "what I ain't gonna do" list:

1. I ain't gonna cook for no man
   ('cause I ain't no slave).

2. I ain't gonna let no man tell me what to do
   ('cause I ain't no child).

3. I ain't gonna clean no house
   ('cause I ain't no maid).

4. I ain't gonna suck that thing
   ('cause I ain't no ho).

Ladies, if you are trying to get into the dating game with any of these hang-ups, you are losing before you begin, and you will be in a perpetual state of frustration.

In order to have a relationship with a *quality* man, a woman must have qualifications and *credentials*. Many women mistake having *credentials* with having *potential*. Everyone has potential. If you play the lottery, you have the potential to win a million dollars. But if you educate yourself, acquire specific knowledge, and master certain business skills, you then will have the credentials to *make* a million dollars.

This is why it is important for women to accumulate bargaining chips. Many women in the dating game make the mistake of relying solely on physical attributes to try and maintain a relationship.

Any woman can *get* a man. But the game a woman has to back up her looks will help her *keep* a man. When a man is first getting to know a woman, he usually puts her into one of two categories:

1. The potential girlfriend category.

2. The potential sex partner category.

Now the requirements for a woman to be placed in the potential girlfriend category vary, depending on a man's particular wants and needs. Before a man places a woman in this category, he looks at her credentials. And the credentials could include a hundred things. A man might take a woman's educational background into consideration. He might consider her culinary skills. He might take her sense of humor, her diet regimen, her sex appeal, or a host of other things into consideration before he puts a woman into the potential girlfriend category.

But it doesn't take much for a man to put a woman into the potential sex partner category. The requirements are minimal. As a matter of fact, a woman just needs to have two things in order to get placed into the potential sex partner category:

1. A poon-tang

2. A pulse

In most cases, when a woman is first dating a man, if she doesn't meet any of his qualifications to become a potential girlfriend or mate, she automatically gets placed in the potential sex partner category.

On the other hand, a woman in most cases actually has to *like* something about a man before she will have sexual relations with him, and she will require him to have certain credentials before she gets physical with him. So a lot of women end up thinking that just because a man wants to sleep with them, he must see some special qualities in her as well. Which brings us to:

Play or Be Played Rule #1

A man does not have to like you to have sex with you.

A very common question that I often hear women ask is, "If a man just wants sex, how come he doesn't just say that in the beginning?" The answer is, most men at least have some *common sense*. Let's be realistic, ladies. Do you honestly think that a man is going to step to you and say "Hey look, I don't really want a relationship with you, I just want to hit that ass?" If he did, you would dismiss him with the quickness. Men know that, so guys at least have enough common sense to know what to say, and what not to say, to get what they want and not salt their own game.

So ladies, it's up to you to figure out what a man's true agenda is, instead of complaining about what he *should* tell you, and what he ought to be doing.

In order to do this, you have to break relationships down to their basic components. There are basically three types of relationships:

1. emotional

2. sexual

3. financial

That's it. There are relationships for emotional gratification, sexual gratification, and financial gratification.

If you are in a relationship with a person, it will be for at least one of these three reasons. The problems come when the two parties have different relationship agendas. A woman may be dating a man because he is paying her bills, and he may be dating her strictly for the sex. Or a woman might be dating a guy whom she's emotionally attached to, while he is dating her because she gives him a couple of dollars every now and then.

In the ideal relationship the two people dating are on the same page emotionally, sexually, and financially. If there is a deficiency in any one of these areas, and the deficiency has not been rectified, the relationship will be temporary. So ladies, when you start dating a man, you must first be real (with yourself especially) about what your true agenda is. If you are dating a man strictly because of his financial contributions, acknowledge that to *yourself.* Don't try to justify your agenda by getting into a BS relationship with the person and deceiving yourself into believing that you can learn to like other qualities about the person.

You must also figure out what the other person's true agenda is. Don't leave it up to them to tell you. In any game, you have to at least play good defense until you are absolutely sure that the other person is willing to be on the same team as you.

When you first meet a person, you can't tell if they are with you or against you. And if someone has plans to get over on you, or to get what they can from you without reciprocating, they damn sure aren't going to tell you this up front.

Over 90 percent of all communication is nonverbal. So it's up to you to look and listen very closely to a person's nonverbal language (and not your own hopes and expectations) so you can figure out where they are coming from.

What Do Men Really Want?

Even though people have unique qualities and characteristics, *all* men have a common thread, and all women have a common thread. Every man has two basic needs: a primal need and a social need. A man's basic primal need is to have an orgasm (I think a lot of you ladies have figured that one out already). And a man's social need is to have power through leadership.

When I say power, I don't mean in an Ike Turner, "sing-the-song-like-I-wrote-it" context. I mean power as far as a man being his own man. I mean power as in being a leader, and not having to conform to anyone. I mean having the power to be the king of his castle. The master of his domain. I mean the power to lead his family in the right direction, and the power to achieve financial freedom.

If a man doesn't utilize his energy to achieve social power, he will settle for just achieving an orgasm. An orgasm gives a man a false sense of power. The basic instinct of every living species is self-preservation. And when a man doesn't have social power, he will resort back to his basic primal need, which is to procreate. And in the mind of a primal thinking man, having an orgasm will ensure his lineage.

Since a man's two basic needs are to have an orgasm and to have power, the level of his game depends on how important one is over the other. Now a man who is disciplined and secure with himself will usually seek out power. But a scrub, or other socially powerless man, will settle for an orgasm.

Now notice I stated that a man's primal need is to have an orgasm, and not just to get coochie (many women erroneously assume that this is basically what all men really want, which causes many women to place a false sense of value on their vaginas). Getting coochie is just the easiest way for a man to *obtain* an orgasm. But some men will settle for oral sex, hand release, or any other thing that will help them reach an orgasm. Some men with extremely low character will literally bang anything that's moist.

In ancient times, when primitive warriors conquered an opposing tribe or city, they would extend their dominance by conquering the women in the form of rape. And many men still have traits of this primitive mentality today.

In the psyche of a primitive-thinking man, using someone to help him achieve an orgasm gives him a perverse sense of victory. This makes him feel dominant and powerful. Some men have such low character, and are so desperate for power, they don't even care who or *what* helps them achieve an orgasm.

This is why some men will have sex with crack whores, animals, underage children, and other men, simply because a female isn't available at the time.

For the record, I'm not knocking the gay *lifestyle*. If a man is living a gay lifestyle, and he is honest with *himself* about it, I have no problem with that. More power to you. You go girl. Do your thing. But, I do have a problem with a guy who is fronting as if he's straight, by acting mackish and gangsta, but on the DL, he will substitute another man's booty for a vagina if he runs out of other options. In the minds of these men, they don't consider themselves gay (this mentality is prevalent with many men who are in prison).

Men like this will compromise all of their integrity, just to bust a nut. These types of men are what I refer to as caveman players.

In my book *The Art of Mackin'*, I pointed out that the terms *pimps, players,* and *macks* are not synonymous or interchangeable. There is a difference between the three. A pimp is a person who is *financially* motivated. A player is a person who is *sexually* motivated. And a mack is a person who is *knowledge and power* motivated. And when a man has knowledge and power, he then has a king's mentality, giving him the option to get sex and money at his whim.

The Difference Between Kings and Cavemen

Thousands of years ago, the Egyptians were the first people to rise above being led by their primal instinct to simply procreate. They utilized that energy to create social order, language, science, and mathematics.

This social structure made it possible for the person who acquired knowledge and power to move higher up on the social totem pole. As evident in the drawings and hieroglyphics left in Egyptian tombs, the men who were more socially powerful received the biggest praise, had more women (or wives), and had more money than the men who had less game.

The Egyptians kings and pharaohs were ancient macks.

In those ancient hieroglyphics, you see them chillin' with three or four women standing by their side. These men were powerful, and they had the respect of their people.

Now, around the same era, in certain European territories, people were still living as primitive cave dwellers.

These cavemen had no game.

They had no social order, no knowledge, and no power. Their main concern was to procreate by any means. Since these cavemen didn't have the game to spit at a female correctly, the only way many of them could get a female was by brute force.

One infamous strategy these cavemen would use involved hiding in the bushes, waiting for a female to walk by, and hitting her on the head with a club. Once the woman was knocked out, the caveman would drag her by her hair into a secluded area, and basically take the coochie.

This was the foundation of Western civilization's approach to man-woman interactions. And even now, guys who have no game, or social power, still use some of these primitive, caveman techniques. There are many examples of how the caveman mentality is prevalent in modern society. One of the most popular TV shows among young men today is *Jackass,* which is simply about a group of men who do a lot of primitive stunts while torturing each other in the process.

The caveman mentality was also clearly seen a few years ago when following the Puerto Rican Day parade in New York, a large group of men rampaged through Central Park, snatching women's clothes off, then dousing the women with water.

If you go to certain nightclubs today, you will see some guys grabbing on women, literally pulling their hair, and making offensive and aggressive remarks to compensate for a lack of verbal game. So it is very important for a woman to learn how to differentiate a king from a caveman player.

The Main Thing Women Should Look For in a Man

As I stated before, one of man's basic needs is to achieve social power. To become the alpha male. In the wild, the male animal who outfights, outhunts, and overpowers the other male animals becomes the dominant male of his group. And by virtue of being the most powerful, he gets the most respect from the other male animals. Plus, most of the female animals want to procreate with the alpha male, because this will ensure the strength of her lineage.

Human males have this competitive nature as well. This is why men are more intrigued with challenging and combative activities such as sports, politics, war, and the stock market. These things give men social challenges to overcome, and overcoming obstacles and stepping up to challenges builds strength that leads to greater social power.

Once a man has overcome certain challenges, this establishes him as being more powerful than those who could not rise to the challenge. And social power makes a man more desirable to women. Many women have acknowledged that power in a man is an aphrodisiac. When a man has power, he doesn't have to chase women. Women chase him. But when a man doesn't have social power, and he isn't making an attempt to achieve social power, he will waste his competitive energy on dominating coochie—on finding challenging ways to achieve an orgasm. So the best way to judge a man is to see what he is doing in life to achieve social power, if he is even trying to achieve power at all. Is he disciplined? Is he educating himself? Is he doing anything constructive? Is he proactive? What is he passionate about? These are the questions a woman should ask herself about a potential partner when she first meets him.

If a man isn't focusing his energy on constructive or proactive social activities, then most likely he will utilize all that energy on getting his next orgasm. And having *power* doesn't necessarily mean being *rich*. Focusing his energy on something he's passionate about makes a man more confident and self-assured. And when people are knowledgeable and thorough about something that they can contribute to society, they have more power. And the thing that a man is passionate about could seem trivial to other people. But all knowledge is a form of potential power, because we never know when certain knowledge may have to be utilized.

It can be any kind of knowledge. Let's take something as far fetched as, say, beekeeping. Now, there isn't a lot of money in beekeeping, but for beekeepers it's their hobby and it's something that they are passionate about. Other people might look at beekeepers and think that they are strange for having such an odd hobby. But a few years ago in California, there were a number of unprecedented cases of wild bees swarming and attacking people and animals. When the authorities couldn't explain where the bees were coming from and why they were becoming so violent, who did they turn to? That's right. The beekeepers. So now the beekeeper that everyone thought was strange, and that everyone ignored, was suddenly the man, and his specialized knowledge helped save a lot of lives.

It's gratifying for a man to know that his expertise can be an asset to society. A man who seeks social power takes great pleasure in knowing that people will come to him to utilize his specialized knowledge. And if his expertise is sought after on a continual basis, his knowledge has the potential to lead to financial gain, and increased power.

Take a guy who is passionate about computers. People might even label him a geek. But if this geek diddles around on his computer, and creates a software program that everyone becomes interested in, as Bill Gates did, and ends up making over $50 billion, all of a sudden he's not a geek anymore. He's now a mack. That's power. Every man wants to be the best at *something,* and every man wants to be the leading authority on something.

This is why actors become directors. Salesmen become CEOs. Athletes become coaches. Because once a man has been through the rigors and the difficulties of gaining skills in something he is passionate about, he gets more passion out of teaching, training, and directing others on what he has learned. This is social power.

Another very important trait that women must look for when selecting a potential mate is leadership skills. In order for a man to be a good leader, or to have others respect him and look to him for guidance, it's imperative that he has integrity.

When a man is being led by other people, he has to conform to the rules and standards of the people he is following.

If a man is working for an employer, he has to follow the rules and regulations of that employer. If a man is still living with his parents, he has to follow the rules and regulations of his parents. If a man is financially dependent on a woman he is dating, he has to follow the rules and regulations of that woman.

In many cases, following the rules and regulations of others causes men to rebel and want to branch out on their own. Now, it's perfectly normal for a man to want to be self-sufficient and call the shots for himself, because following the rules and standards of others will often limit a person from growing to his fullest potential. But when you become a social "free agent," you have to be disciplined enough to set rules and standards for *yourself*. This is the basic definition of integrity, and the presence of integrity separates the kings from the cavemen.

It's in a woman's nature to seek leadership in a man, because leadership represents strength. However, this natural instinct causes many women to gravitate toward men who are considered bad boys or thugs, because many men who are considered rebels give off the *illusion* of leadership.

Anyone can rebel just for the sake of rebelling, so when a man rebels, he should do so in a way that credits his character with integrity. This is an important quality for women to look for in a man. If a man wants to be self-sufficient because he doesn't want any limitations on how high he wants to rise, that's perfectly fine. But having integrity will also ensure that he puts limitations on how low he can sink.

Sports and entertainment are two of the very few occupations in which a person can become extremely successful without the foundation of integrity; and this is why many very successful athletes and entertainers get into trouble with the law.

If a man is to be successful in his position as the president of a Fortune 500 company, he has to have enough integrity to lead employees to handle their duties and responsibilities with an equal level of integrity. But you don't need integrity or leadership skills in order to dribble a ball or write a hit song.

So a lot of ball players, rappers, and singers will use their talents to rise to the top of their field, but many of them will jeopardize it all by getting into trouble over dumb shit that could have easily been avoided. This is why it is essential for a man to have integrity. And this is the main thing that women should look for in a man.

Tip #1 on how women can have game:

*Be a queen by always taking full responsibility
for your actions and decisions.*

No one respects a professional victim, and no man wants to invest in a woman who blames everyone else for her mistakes, because men know that sooner or later, that woman will be blaming *them* for something. Plus, it shows good character when a woman can take responsibility for her actions and acknowledge any mistakes she might have made. This shows she is willing to improve herself, and reflects a king's own desire to constantly improve himself, and build on his existing knowledge.

2: What Women Really Want

Men have been trying to figure out what women want for centuries; and, if they're honest, it's a question that women have long been trying to figure out as well. Even Sigmund Freud, the father of modern psychoanalysis, went to the grave without being able to figure out: *"What do women want?"*

Well, those of us in the hustling community have figured it out, and for the first time in the history of the written word, the answer will be printed—right here, in the pages of this book. It is extremely important that women know the answer to this question, because this will help women get a better understanding of why they instinctively do certain things, and why they choose or don't choose certain dating partners.

As much as women may hate to be categorized, there is a common thread that connects all women. Just like men, all women have a primal need and a social need. A woman's primal need is to get attention, and her social need is to get appreciation. And attention for a woman is the equivalent of an orgasm for a man.

Just as some men will get desperate and do anything for an orgasm, some women will get desperate and do anything for attention. As I stated before, a man's basic primal need is to have an orgasm in order to procreate. A woman can have orgasms all day long, but that's not going to help her procreate. Therefore, a woman's basic primal goal is to get *attention* in order to be *chosen* for procreation. And the level of a woman's game will determine whom she will procreate with.

In most species, the females compete to see who will get the attention from, and who will procreate with, the alpha male. The female of the species understands that obtaining the seed of the alpha male will help ensure the strength of her lineage. If the female chooses a weaker male, she will get a weaker seed. And getting a weaker seed makes it more likely for her to have a weaker offspring.

In the wild, the females of some species will give off certain scents, or make certain types of physical gestures in order to get attention from the males. The strongest female lions, with the most hunting skills, get the attention of the dominant male. This same process is evident in human social behavior. Women who are more attractive, disciplined, physically fit, and about their hustle are more likely to attract ballers. And women who are lazy, uneducated, and undisciplined are more likely to attract scrubs. This is why it is important for women to do things they can be appreciated for. This is what helps define a woman.

Too many women define themselves based on their physical attributes, and will settle for getting attention rather than being appreciated. As their physical attributes fade over time, women who have defined themselves by looks lose their sense of identity when they get older, and this causes them to become depressed or bitter. Thus it is very important for a woman to have game to back up her looks, and not just settle for getting short-term attention.

Any female can get attention from a man. Hell, if you put a gorilla in a G-string and take it to a club, I guarantee that some guy will buy it a drink.

The Difference Between Leadership and Nurturing

Unlike men, women aren't as concerned with the power of being a leader. Contrary to most feminist teachings, it's not in a woman's nature to be the leader of the family or a relationship.

Women are generally excellent nurturers, and in this modern society, many people have confused nurturing for leadership. Most women are emotional thinkers (you know you are, ladies, let's keep it real) and emotions can literally change with the weather. A very popular philosophy in our culture is, "It's a woman's prerogative to change her mind." Well, this philosophy alone weakens any prospect of leadership skills a person is supposed to have.

If you are a leader, and you have other people following you, you can't have this philosophy. When other people are depending on your leadership for their well-being, it is *not* your prerogative to change your mind. To be a leader, you have to be definitive in your statements and actions, and you have to be able to follow through with any plans you make. Once people see that you are not 100 percent thorough with your leadership, they will not put you in a position of power. You can't be the head of a corporation and tell your employees,

"I'm sorry I couldn't make it to the meeting yesterday, because I was upset, so I changed my mind." Think about what this would do for the morale of your workers.

Even though there are exceptions, most women simply don't want the responsibility of power and leadership. Since having leadership power goes against a woman's very nature, women who are given too much of this power will oftentimes abuse and misuse it.

Almost every woman who has been in the workplace has worked at a job where there was a female supervisor who got into little catty power struggles with other female employees. Ladies, you all have known a female boss or superior who would reprimand someone for some petty, nit-picky bullshit, simply to flex her authority. Sure there are male supervisors, too, who will sometimes abuse their authority, but for the most part, male bosses are more concerned with company productivity than bringing up small, petty issues in order to show people who's the boss. But businesses with a number of female supervisors, such as hair salons and beauty shops, are breeding grounds for catty power struggles between women.

I have known many female hairdressers who have gone from shop to shop, changing employment venues because they couldn't get along with other female employees or female shop owners. Again, like I said, there are many exceptions to this rule. There are powerful women who *are* leaders. There are women out there who have worked to climb the corporate ladder to success. And there are women who are fair and just with their power and authority. But most women who set out to achieve social power and leadership do so out of necessity. As I stated before, people are generally opportunists. When they are trying to achieve a certain goal, they will normally take the easiest path available to them.

If a woman really wants to be financially set in life, she has every opportunity in the world to become the next Oprah. Not only are there opportunities, there are incentives and programs to get women into colleges and other academic institutions. And as easy as it is to file lawsuits in this country these days, most major corporations wouldn't dare discriminate against a woman who was more qualified than a man for a particular position. The reality is, many women don't go for climbing the corporate ladder by obtaining power through leadership, because many of them would rather attract the *attention* of a man who is financially successful instead of going through the trials and tribulations of becoming successful themselves. The women who say "well, I make my own money," and "I don't need a man to pay my bills," are usually the females who *can't* get a man to pay their bills.

Very attractive women usually have men offer them things, and most women will take advantage of these opportunities. This doesn't make them bad people, they are just utilizing their options. Women who don't have the looks to get a man to offer them things have basically two options:

1. Starve

2. Get things on their own

Again, people are opportunists and will generally utilize the options given to them. This is true with both men and women.

Men who claim that they would never have relationships with multiple women are usually men who don't have the game or the power to get multiple women. When a person doesn't have options, it's easy for him to try to hide behind moral smoke screens. Men who have power and influence can get multiple women, and many of them *do* have relationships with multiple women at the same time. If you have any doubt about this, think about the most powerful, influential male leaders of the last fifty years. All of them had player tendencies. This didn't make them bad people. They just had it like that. Men like John F. Kennedy . . . great man . . . he had multiple women. Martin Luther King . . . great man . . . he had multiple women. Elijah Muhammad . . . great man . . . he had multiple women. Bill Cosby, Muhammed Ali, Michael Jordan, Jesse Jackson, and Bill Clinton are all great men, and they all have had multiple women. The list could go on and on.

These men changed the face of modern society, and the fact that they utilized their options doesn't take away from the validity of their greatness.

Offer the *average* attractive female two choices on how to come up: either (1) go to school, get your degree, and work your way up the financial ladder; or (2) put on that dress that makes your ass look nice, and hang around some ballers.

Which choice do you think the *average* female will make? She will take the easy route because it's human nature to take the easiest route to a desired destination. Now an *exceptional* female, who is attractive enough to get men to trick off paper for her, will rise above the instant gratification of making the quick buck. She will choose the long-term benefits of self-achieved success. Again, this is what an *exceptional* woman will do, and there are but a few exceptional men and women in the world.

Everyone wants to have a sense of empowerment. For men, becoming a leader is empowering; for women, doing something that they are appreciated for is empowering. The problem is, society tries to teach women to transform their nurturing instincts into leadership skills.

For a person to have a better chance of surviving in the world, he or she needs leadership *and* nurturing. This is why having both parents is very important in the lives of children. Now men are *capable* of nurturing, but it's more natural for women to play that role (this is why women are more likely to be given custody of children in most divorce cases). Women are *capable* of being leaders in relationships, but it's more natural for men to play that role.

Since society tells women things like "you don't need a man" and "you can have children, and be the mama and the daddy," many women try to transform their nurturing skills into a false sense of leadership. And leadership and nurturing are two different things. Children need nurturing from their mothers to strengthen and build them up. Once they have the strength and nurturing they need from mother, they then need the leadership, guidance, and direction of a *father figure* to really break the game of life down to them. A man can better give his children advice on the consequences of their actions in the real world. See, women have more of a cushion to be in denial about certain things in life. But the consequences of a man's actions are more swift and immediate. A woman, for example, can afford to date the wrong type of man, over and over again. Even though she might accumulate a lot of emotional baggage from doing this, her physical well-being will pretty much stay intact. But a man can't afford to date the wrong women over and over again. If a man messes up and dates *one* wrong woman, the next thing you know, his paycheck is getting garnished. So this cause-and-effect pattern generally teaches men the lessons of life much faster. Society basically forces men to face reality. Being in denial, for a man, is rarely an option.

By the time many women learn the consequences of life's

actions, they oftentimes have a sense of bitterness attached to the knowledge. Because most likely, these women had to repeatedly go through some shit in order to finally "get it."

Nowadays, many young ladies have relationship issues because they didn't have a father figure to really lace them with the game. Many single mothers do the best they can to break the game down, but for the most part, they can only give nurturing advice on dealing with relationships.

If you ask the average mother for advice on your relationship problems, she's likely to tell you to "pray on it" or "just leave it in the hands of the Lord." When it comes to dealing with relationship issues or any other life problems, you need specific advice strategies, and directions on how to overcome these problems. Nurturing advice is helpful, but it's not enough.

Giving people nurturing without leadership is like building a car with just a gas tank and no steering wheel. A car needs a filled gas tank to run properly—to give the car power and energy. But the car also needs a steering wheel to guide it properly. Without a steering wheel, the car will just drive around in circles until it runs out of gas. And many people who lack direction find themselves running around in circles, wasting "gas" or energy that, with the proper direction, could be used on more constructive endeavors.

The Making of a Queen

In every relationship, the man and woman each have their own role. If a man is staying home with the kids while the woman is out working, many *women* will feel that the man isn't playing his role. And if the woman is the leader in the relationship, she is not playing her natural role. This isn't empowering to women, and it isn't empowering to the relationship.

The first women in the world to become socially empowered were the ancient Egyptian queens. These women didn't gain power because they were leaders, they got it for the way they had the backs of their *kings*. Egyptian queens such as Nefertiti, Isis, and Hatshepsut were admired and appreciated by the masses for the way they held up the integrity, philosophies, and principles of their families.

The woman is the *foundation* of the family. And if the foundation of the family is unstable, the family won't stand a chance in the time of crisis. But if there is a strong female figure acting as the backbone of the family, the family unit will be able to overcome any obstacles that they may have.

Even in modern times, women are still admired and appreciated for the way they hold their families together. Most popular female icons gained popularity with the masses in this way. When JFK was assassinated, his widow, Jackie, was universally admired for keeping her family unit intact with strength and courage. Princess Diana was one of the most popular and loved women in the world. She wasn't a leader, nor did she try to be. She was a compassionate and nurturing person, who always held up the integrity of the royal family.

Hillary Clinton became extremely popular after people saw how she held it down for her family, when Bill Clinton was slippin'. Hillary's role as the family's backbone was very important, because if she could forgive Bill and continue to have faith in him to atone for his indiscretions, the general public felt that they could forgive him as well. This is one of the reasons why Bill Clinton maintained his popularity with the public throughout his scandals. Bill remained a *king*, because he had a strong *queen* right there to back him up.

An example of what can happen when a family unit has a weak female foundation can be found in the relationship between Jim and Tammy Faye Baker. Jim was a weak leader, and Tammy Faye was an even weaker foundation. The Bakers had a multimillion-dollar television ministry, when Jim became caught up in a sex scandal, then consequently a financial scandal. When Jim was about to be indicted on charges, and the family ministry was in jeopardy, the media wanted to get a reaction from Tammy Faye. Instead of keeping it together, being strong, and holding her head up for her family, Tammy Faye appeared on every news channel in the country, crying and blubbering, with her mascara running down her face. Jim looked like a fool, and Tammy Faye looked like a straight clown. She became a punchline in the media and popular culture at the time. And when Jim was convicted and sent to prison, Tammy Faye *ran* and got a divorce from Jim before he could even get his prison suit on. Then she went and married one of Jim's friends. Their ministry fell off. Jim fell off. Their teenage daughter ran away from home and became estranged from the family. Basically, their family fell off.

Even though Tammy Faye tried to distance herself from Jim and the scandal by playing the "I-didn't-know-what-was-going-on" role, she still became a laughingstock and in the end, no one bought her attempt at redemption. The public is not going to invest faith in a person with a history of instability.

If you distance yourself from your own family in the midst of a crisis, people will imagine what you will do to them, and will respond accordingly. There is a diplomatic way and an emotional way to handle any problem or crisis. A queen will always handle a situation with diplomacy and integrity. This is how she earns respect and appreciation.

The Compassionate Mother
vs. the All-Knowing Mammy

Throughout history, the women who have received the most appreciation are those who have the most wisdom, life experiences, and compassion for those around them. This is especially true for the black community.

Back in the day, every black community had a compassionate mother figure that everyone in the neighborhood respected and looked to for nurturing. These sistas would go out of their way to help everyone in their community. These were the *real* grandmothers. I'm not talking about these thirty-nine-year-old grandmothers we have today. I'm talking about Big Mama. Nana. Muh-Dear. Those real, true-to-the-game grandmothers held it down for the community, and they earned the respect and appreciation of all of the people around them.

Unfortunately, the image of the compassionate mother has been transformed into the image of the all-knowing mammy. The stereotypical mammy commonly comes in the form of the overweight, nonthreatening, sassy, know-it-all black woman who is always willing to put someone in check. The mammy image has always been comforting to the American public. Whenever the television viewing audience has problems, they know they can always turn on that image of mammy to make everything all right.

The all-knowing mammy has always been a staple of movies, sitcoms, and daytime talk shows. Hattie McDaniel in *Gone with the Wind*. Florida Evans from *Good Times*. Shirley and Mama from the TV show *What's Happenin'*. Nell Carter. Mother Love. Monique from *The Parkers*. Queen Latifah. Thea Vidale. Star Jones. Judge Mablean Ephriam from the TV show *Divorce Court.* And Ms. "You told Harpo to beat me" herself, Oprah Winfrey.

Speaking of Oprah, I have to give her the props she deserves. For a while Oprah was the epitome of the mammy stereotype. (Her role as Ms. Sophia in *The Color Purple* was mammyism at its best). Unlike the other mammys, Oprah had the insight and discipline to rise above that mammy image, and transform herself back into a compassionate and nurturing personality that deserves respect and appreciation.

Oprah decided to make an effort to control her weight, and she made a choice to stop doing the male-bashing, women-as-victims topics on her show. This helped make Oprah one of the most powerful women in television. The good thing about Oprah is that she didn't abuse this power by trying to be something she isn't. She didn't try to come across as a leader, or a New Age guru, who gives people half-assed advice. Oprah comes across as a person who will listen to your problems without passing judgment. And she chose to use her show as a forum to get people who were knowledgeable about specific topics to give their insight.

Oprah was wise enough to play the sideline and bring on people like Dr. Phil and John Gray to give their expertise on relationships and life issues. Oprah has acquired the basic qualities of a queen's mentality. She does what she can to assist people and to give them wisdom. If she isn't familiar with a particular problem or subject, instead of trying to be a know-it-all, and giving people the wrong advice, she is woman enough to find people who are more qualified than she is.

Not all women who are in a position of power have the integrity to humble themselves when they aren't knowledgeable about a particular subject. Take for example, some of the token mammies who have been in the media spotlight, such as

Ricki Lake and Rosie O'Donnell. These women don't earn the respect that Oprah does, because they constantly try to lend their expertise on subjects that they are clearly not qualified for.

When Ricki Lake does her show, it would be best if she would remain neutral, and let the guests on the panel reveal and resolve their issues. Instead, Ricki always has to throw her two cents in, making useless comments such as "Girl!. You need to kick him to the curb," and "You can do better than him," or a number of other played-out catchphrases.

The thing about Ricki Lake is she knows she's a token mammy. She knows she is running game on her audience. And she keeps her subject matter lighthearted for the most part.

These are just a few examples of women who gain power through leadership instead of women gaining power through appreciation. And again, there are many exceptions. The bottom line is, most women don't even want power through leadership. Many women might say they want this kind of power, because it's a popular stance to take around certain feminist-influenced circles. But men and women generally want to embody themselves with things that attract the opposite sex. Most women are attracted to a man who has social power. Like I said before, many women have acknowledged that power in a man is an aphrodisiac. And this gives men the incentive to become financially successful in life.

When a man lists the qualities he wants in a woman, power usually isn't on the list. Generally, the first item is physical attractiveness, with things like nurturing skills and intelligence coming second and third on the list. This gives women the incentive to become more attractive to men.

Men aren't as concerned with their own physical attributes because they know that power will compensate for any physical shortcomings. We have all seen beautiful women literally *flock* around unattractive male entertainers and athletes, simply because these men had power. But you will never see a group of men flocking around WNBA players. Either men find women attractive, or they don't. When a woman has her shit together, that's the *icing* on the cake. But a woman's power or independence has no bearing on a man's initial decision to step to a female.

Men are physical creatures. And we are generally intrigued by things that pique our physical interest. So women should remember:

Played or Be Played Rule #2

A female's ability to attract attention
will *get* a man, but what a woman does
to receive appreciation will *keep* a man.

When a woman has a skill that she can be appreciated for, she has acquired game. I'll discuss what some of these skills are in chapter 11, "How to Become a Queen."

How the Need for Attention Is the Root of Most Female Behavior

Appreciation is a positive form of attention; and as I stated before, when a woman isn't doing anything to be appreciated for, she will resort to just getting attention. And the less game a woman has, the more in need of attention she will become.

As I stated before, attention for a woman is the equivalent

of an orgasm for a man. Some men with no game will do anything for an orgasm. And some women with no game will do anything for attention. For example, a man can go on a date with a woman he doesn't like, just so he can achieve an orgasm. And women will go on dates with men they don't like, just to get the attention. Men aren't as concerned with attention as women are. And women aren't as concerned with getting an orgasm as men are.

When men go out to places like nightclubs, they are generally not concerned with just getting attention. You'll see most of the guys playing the background or posted up against the wall, scouting for females. The ultimate goal for a man going to a nightclub is to acquire a potential sex partner. And if he can get one *that night*, that makes it that much better. Some men will *settle* for a dance or a phone number, but a man's main goal is to find a woman who will help him achieve an orgasm at the end of the night.

Now women, on the other hand, will go to the club *strictly* to get some attention. Females will spend long hours on their clothes, hair, shoes, and makeup, go out to the club and not talk to anyone there, and totally be satisfied at the end of the night.

Some women will dress extremely stank, just to have a group of guys ogle over them. Getting this form of attention gives women a false sense of confidence and a temporary ego boost. Some women don't even care if the attention is positive or negative. We've all seen hoochies at the club, wearing loud animal prints, too much makeup, and ghetto hairstyles, getting drunk and grinding on a number of men (and women). Some women literally act like wild animals, simply to get attention. And the only men who hunt or chase after wild animals are cavemen.

So it is very important for a woman to set high standards for herself, because the petty victory of getting caveman attention shouldn't be what validates her self-worth. A woman should never vie for male attention if it will compromise her integrity and self-respect. Because even though people will accept you, that doesn't mean they will respect you.

A man might meet a woman at a club, and she might agree to have sex with him that night. Even though he may accept sex from her, most likely he won't respect her as far as being a long-term mate. And a woman might meet a guy whom she is not even remotely attracted to, but he may offer to take her on an expensive date, and to shower her with gifts. Even though the woman might accept the gifts and the date, she probably won't respect him the same way she would a non-trick.

Some men are more intrigued by a woman if she makes him *earn* an orgasm. And some women are more intrigued by a man who makes her *earn* his attention. Ladies, you all have dealt with a guy who gave you a little *too* much attention, or too much attention *too soon.* You know . . . that bugaboo brotha who called you twenty times a day, or the guy who wanted to be up under you all the time. Nothing turns a woman off more than a man who gives her too much attention by jumping up whenever she snaps her fingers. A man like this doesn't challenge a woman. And many women want a man who is somewhat of a challenge because meeting challenges gives you growth and experience.

And when you have the challenge of getting a man who has his shit together, or a man with king characteristics, you have to be strong enough and woman enough to rise to that challenge.

When I say strong enough, I don't mean you should have a domineering and combative attitude toward the man. I mean that after you get his attention, you are going to have to upgrade your game to get his appreciation.

Attention Freaks

Attention freaks are the female equivalent of the caveman players. Attention freaks try to get attention any way they can. These women are also referred to as spotlight freaks. The four main types of attention freaks are:

1. The hoochie

2. The drama queen

3. The hypochondriac

4. The professional victim

Here's a rundown of the four types:

The Hoochie

The hoochie is the most common attention freak. The hoochie female is desperate for male attention, and she will dress in loud or skimpy clothes to get it.

The hoochie will mutilate her body in order to get male attention. She will have breast implants and all sorts of other cosmetic surgeries, tongue rings and nipple piercings and all types of tattoos.

Many hoochies will pair up with other attention freaks, and go to clubs where a lot of men are, and they will play the bisexual role in front of the men, just to get attention. At almost every popular club nowadays, you will see at least two females on the dance floor, humping and grinding on each other. And there will be a crowd of cavemen standing around them, watching their performance. Hoochies live to have a male audience. This is why many hoochies are strippers. Many people assume that hoochies strip for the money, but contrary to popular belief, most strippers don't make that much money (all those $1 tips don't add up to much at the end of the night, unless the stripper is doing "extras"). Most females who strip do it for the attention, not for the money.

We live in a society where people want their needs met immediately. And hoochies would rather have the instant gratification of caveman attention, instead of the long-term accomplishments of a *king's appreciation*.

The Drama Queen

The drama queen is the attention freak who always puts extras on shit. She blows every little issue way out of proportion in order to bring attention to herself. The drama queen lives in her own little self-delusional world where everything is more hectic than it really is. And she feels a great sense of power when she can reel others into her drama-filled world.

Drama queens usually live very mediocre and boring lives, and they have a lot of idle time on their hands, so they feel that they have to create a make-believe world full of drama and excitement. In the mind of the drama queen, drama is better than boredom.

Some of the logic that drama queens use can be so far-fetched that it borders on the insane. When a particular subject or person is mentioned in the presence of a drama queen, she will often try to find a way to associate herself with the topic, in order to become the center of attention. For instance, if a Laker game is being shown on TV, the drama queen might say something like "Girl, Kobe Bryant tried to talk to me." Or if a person walks into the room with a particular outfit on, the drama queen might say something like "Nobody was wearing Gucci, until *I* started wearing Gucci. Why are all these girls trying to be like me?" And the sad thing is, these drama queens are dead serious when they use this self-delusional rhetoric.

The Hypochondriac

The hypochondriac is an attention freak who creates imaginary physical ailments in order to receive attention through sympathy. Hypochondriacs are usually middle-aged women who are overweight, and they like to use their make-believe symptoms as conversation starters. If you ask a hypochondriac a simple question like "How have you been?" she will start fishing for sympathy by going into a long spiel about how her legs hurt, she's been having migraines, her back is acting up again, and her hemorrhoids are itching like crazy.

The Professional Victim

The professional victim is another attention freak who tries to get attention through sympathy. In the mind of a professional victim, everyone is out to do her wrong. And she refuses to take any responsibility for the choices she makes in life.

The professional victim blames everybody else for everything bad in her life. If she becomes a drug user, she will claim it's because her mother didn't hug her as a child. If she is an alcoholic, she will say it's not her fault, because alcoholism runs in her family. If she has a number of children at a young age, she will claim it's because guys keep getting her pregnant.

Oftentimes, this type of attention freak will purposely put herself in situations that would place her in the position of being a victim. The professional victim will seek out relationships with lowlifes and losers, then complain that all her relationships are abusive.

This type of female creates a negative cycle, because no one respects a professional victim. And most people try to avoid them at all cost, thus giving the professional victim more reason to feel alienated and victimized.

So ladies, this is why it is very important for you not just to avoid being an attention freak, but to make a conscious decision to do something productive that you can be appreciated for. Because if you just relax and sit still, and do nothing at all, the negative impact of just wanting attention will *automatically* take over your consciousness.

Remember, if you are satisfied and content with just getting attention, most likely you are going to attract only cavemen. But if you are ready to upgrade your game, and stop interacting with cavemen, you have to stop hanging out in caves. You can't be in the raunchiest nightclubs in town, looking for marriage material. If you want a king, you have to start hanging out in castles. Now going to a castle is one thing, but once you get inside a castle, you have to look and act like you *belong* there (you can't go to a lawyers' convention wearing purple braids and ten tattoos). A king can spot an outsider from a mile away, and this is why you have to elevate yourself to queen status. A queen doesn't have to *try* to get attention from others to validate her self-worth, because a queen already knows she's the shit. And when you are the shit, you can adapt and relate to anyone in any environment.

Tip #2 on how women can have game:

Try to smile as much as you can.

When a person smiles, not only does it put them in a better mood; it puts the people around them in a better mood as well. Nowadays, many women go to social gatherings and try their best *not* to smile. Here's the real deal, ladies: walking around with a "mean mug" look on your face does not make you look like a diva. It makes you look like a psycho. So don't be afraid to smile. It makes you more appealing, plus it makes people more comfortable around you.

3: The Different Types of Men

Every man is a mack. Bottom line. Point blank. And if he's not a mack, he wants to be one. It just depends on what level of the game he's in. See ladies, there are different *degrees* of macks. There are **first-degree macks, second-degree macks,** and **third-degree macks.** And it's your job, ladies, to figure out what degree mack your man (or potential man) is.

Now I know when you hear the word *mack,* you automatically think of a man who goes around deceiving women. This is not always the case. This is why there are different degrees of mackin'.

Remember, a mack is a man who has accumulated the knowledge and the power to have the option to get sex and money at his disposal. And ladies, if you honestly think a man doesn't want this type of power, you shouldn't even be in the dating game.

A **first-degree mack** is what a man becomes when he first starts dating. Many first-degree macks don't even know they are macks yet. When a guy begins playing the dating game, he wants to know how to get more women, or how to get *better* women. A first-degree mack might have the best woman in the world right under his nose. But because he's not experienced in his knowledge of women, and he doesn't fully understand the game, he can't see that he has the best woman already. (This is why certain men become successful later on in life, and then go back and marry their high school sweethearts.)

A **second-degree mack** *knows* that he is a mack. And he knows how to spit game at a number of different women who are able to satisfy whatever needs he has. Unfortunately, the second-degree mack often limits his mackin' skills to relationships with women.

The **third-degree mack** uses his mackin' skills not only in his relations with women, but in every other aspect of his life. The third-degree mack knows how to utilize his skills in the business world, the political world, the financial world, and everywhere else.

And when it comes to dealing with females, a third-degree mack is knowledgeable and seasoned enough to look for *quality* instead of *quantity*. He knows that having one top-notch female is better than having twenty chickenheads.

Now, to help women better understand men, I have broken the different types of men down to four major categories. And within these categories, there are several sub-categories. Even though there are exceptions (very few), this list will give you a pretty accurate analysis of the different types of men out there. The four major categories of men are what I call *the four Ps*. They are:

1. Players

2. Professionals

3. Pushovers

4. Parolees

There are positive and negative aspects to all of the four Ps. Here is a rundown.

Players

Players are usually charismatic guys who have the gift of gab when it comes to dealing with the ladies. Players are sexually driven, and they usually need a number of women to satisfy their lustful appetites.

Seasoned players learn how to say the right thing at the right time to the women they are pursuing. This is why women are secretly intrigued by players. Some players are a little more deceptive than others. There are five basic subcategories of the player:

The Smooth Player

The smooth player is the very laid back, nonchalant type of player. He doesn't chase women so much as they chase him. He knows how to position himself to be approached by the type of women he knows can satisfy his needs.

Whenever the smooth player has problems with any of his females, he knows how to sweet-talk them into reconciliation. The smooth player takes great pride in his physical appearance, and usually wears all of the latest, fly, namebrand attire.

His smooth, charismatic personality is magnetic to the women around him, and it's hard to stay mad at the smooth player for long. He puts so much of his sexual energy and passion into his words that he is very convincing when spitting game to the ladies.

The smooth player is very selective in the type of women he will spit at. Many smooth players like to be showered with gifts from the women they deal with (many gigolos start off as smooth players), and they usually won't be bothered with females who can't bring something to the table.

The Gambling Player

The gambling player is the most deceptive of all the players. When it comes to dating, the gambling player has a Vegas mentality. To him, trying to have sex with a number of women is like a dice game. When you roll dice, everything depends on the luck of the throw. And when you are playing, you don't know whether you are going to win or lose. This is what is so intriguing and addictive about gambling, and when a gambling player goes out with a female, he doesn't know whether he is going to have sex with her or not. If he does happen to have sex with a female, he refers to it as "getting lucky."

Most gambling players are not concerned with getting easy sex. If a woman walked up to the average gambling player, and simply offered him easy sex with no strings attached, he probably wouldn't be interested. The gambling player needs to feel that he manipulated the woman out of sex.

If a Vegas type of gambler was rolling dice for fun, and the dice were fixed to win every time, this would take the excitement out of gambling. It's the same with the gambling player. If he knew the outcome of all his encounters with women, that would take the thrill out of it.

The Teenage Player

The teenage player is the guy who will pretty much take whatever he can get. This is mainly because he has a lack of options and bargaining chips. The teenage male is usually still living at home with his parents. He has no car yet. No career yet. And no money yet. So this alone limits his options of females he can talk to. This is why the teenage player is reduced to having relationships only with the local hoodrats in his immediate vicinity (if he's lucky).

The teenage player is at his sexual peak, so every woman he meets is a potential sex partner. The teenage player will lower his standards and show *any* female some attention, as long as he thinks he can get some ass later on down the line. This results in many teenage players being manipulated by women. And when a teenage player gets older, and starts to accumulate bargaining chips to get women, he may have a cynical view of certain women because of the way they treated him as a teenager.

The Caveman Player

The caveman player is the overly aggressive guy who likes to pull and grab on women, then curse them out when he doesn't get no play. Many caveman players are short in stature, and suffer from a Napoleonic complex.

This kind of guy will yell out of his car window at women while he's driving down the street, or make lewd remarks disguised as pick-up lines. The caveman player uses this aggressive, primitive behavior as a defense mechanism, because of his intense fear of rejection. He knows he has no game, so he will purposely produce a negative reaction from females by insulting them before they insult him in the form of rejection.

Then he can justify his failure by claiming that the female was a bitch or she was stuck up.

At one point in his life, the caveman player tried to come at females with a smoother approach, but he probably encountered the wrong female who reacted negatively to him anyway. So the caveman player decided to take the extreme opposite approach from that point on.

The Retro Old-School Player

The retro old-school player is the middle-aged cat who never upgraded to the mack level. Every player must evolve, but the retro old-school player became too complacent in his player stage. So now he just likes to relish the past.

Macks focus more on money, and *players* focus more on poon-tang. A player can spend his time focusing on poon-tang as much as he wants, but at the end of the day, the rent still needs to be paid.

Older, retro players don't share the same long-term success as an older mack. Many old-school players like to reminisce about how they had it going on back in the '70s. There are many ways to spot a retro old-school player. Many retro players have a look that reminds you of Jerome from the TV show *Martin,* and many old-school players are referred to by their first and middle names.

When you meet a brotha with a name like "Charlie Earl," or "Eddie Lee," or "Jimmy Ray," chances are he is a retro old-school player.

Here are the top four ways to tell if a man is a retro old-school player:

1. He still wears a number of herringbone necklaces.

2. He wears Adidas sweat suits with church shoes.

3. He refers to women as "bad mama jammas."

4. He wears a life-alert bracelet with diamonds in it.

Professionals

The professional brotha is usually the very well educated guy who is articulate and goal oriented. He is usually the suit-and-tie type of brotha, who is used to the finer things in life. The professional brotha usually comes from a stable family background, went to the best schools, and usually has his finances in order. There are four basic subcategories of the professional:

The Bourgie Brotha

The bourgie brotha is usually light skinned (though there are many exceptions) and he takes great pride in his mixed ethnicity. The bourgie brotha often comes across as being snobby, and higher than mighty, and he feels his educational background makes him superior to others around him.

The bourgie brotha is his own biggest fan, and he takes great delight in bragging about his accomplishments. You will often hear him say things like "I got my master's degree at Harvard," and "I just purchased the new Lexus," and so on. The bourgie brotha is an extreme narcissist, and it would be hard to convince him that he's not the center of the universe.

The Married Mack

The married mack was once a teenage player, who upgraded his game once he got older. See, the average man doesn't become a real player until he is in his late twenties or early thirties. Like I said before, a teenage player doesn't really have anything to offer a woman. That's why he usually dates hoodrats.

But when a man gets out of college, or gets a real career going, he is usually in his mid to late twenties. At this point, he can get a nicer car, nicer clothes, and a nice crib. Now that he has some bargaining chips, he now has different options as far as getting different types of females.

And when a man gets options, he usually wants to utilize them. The problem with the married mack is that he got married while he was in his teenage player stage. As a teenage player, he was so grateful to the first halfway decent female to give him some play that he wanted to marry her right away.

As the teenage player got older, he started to get his career on track, and to get his finances in order. Now that he has become a professional brotha, he is starting to get play from women who didn't give him play before. So he decides that he is going to stay married, but live a double life, and have his fun with the hoochies on the side.

The Sugar Daddy

The sugar daddy is like a married mack, but on another level. Most married macks are between the ages of twenty-six and thirty-five. Most sugar daddies are between the ages of forty and fifty-five (most white sugar daddies are between the ages of fifty-five and seventy-five. This is because black men in our society have a shorter life span).

Most married macks have women on the side for recreational purposes, but the sugar daddy has women on the side for *control* purposes. The sugar daddy feels a great sense of power by having his chicks on the side (or COTS) dependent upon him. His professional attitude and sense of establishment are what draws women to him (the most common occupation for a sugar daddy is car salesman).

Women who didn't have a father figure in their lives are attracted to the sugar daddy. Also, these women like the competition of trying to take a married man away from his wife.

The sugar daddy uses the façade of generosity to lure women into his trap. Now, before you think of these women as victims, you have to understand that they are usually superficial women, who deserve what they get. Many women who go for sugar daddies are the fast-life type of women, such as strippers, or women who are used to manipulating men. And a lot of females like this think they are getting over on the sugar daddy, because he is showering them with gifts. But a seasoned sugar daddy will up the ante, by giving his COTS a car (in his name) and an apartment (also in his name). And he will keep giving her these things until she becomes totally dependent upon him.

The COTS will think she's gotten over, until she realizes that the sugar daddy isn't ever going to leave his wife. He's going to continue to go back and forth between his wife, the main COTS, and any other woman he pleases. And the COTS won't be able to have a relationship with anyone, because she can't have other men in the apartment that the sugar daddy's paying for. And she can't have other guys in the car that the sugar daddy's paying for, because if she does, she knows her sugar daddy will snatch everything away from her, and then she will be ass-out.

Some COTS will become disenchanted with being in a situation just to provide sex, and they will request more out of the relationship. Sometimes a COTS will try to get her sugar daddy to invest in a business that she is trying to start up (which he doesn't). He knows that the COTS has a shelf life, and when she begins to be too much of a burden, or if the sex plays out, he will simply replace her with another COTS.

Some COTS will become disgruntled, and try to blackmail the sugar daddy by threatening to tell his wife about the affair. But a seasoned sugar daddy knows how to sever all connections between his wife and the COTS. He knows not to give out his home number, and he knows not to tell other women where he lives.

The Evil Genius

The evil genius is the professional who feels that he doesn't receive enough positive affirmations for his work. This constant lack of appreciation and lack of power cause the evil genius to become bitter and frustrated. When certain men acquire a lot of knowledge, and they don't utilize that knowledge in a constructive manner, the knowledge oftentimes turn into negative energy.

We often hear the term, "knowledge is power," but this is not quite true. Knowledge is *potential* power. Utilizing knowledge is like using gas in your home. When gas is handled in a controlled, constructive manner, you can use it to heat up your stove, heat up the room temperature, or heat up your shower water. But if you just turn on your stove, and let gas fumes fill up your house, you have a potentially dangerous scenario. If you have uncontrolled gas fumes floating around your home, there is a possibility that your crib will explode.

It's the same thing with men who have acquired a lot of knowledge, but who have no constructive outlets to use that knowledge.

The problem with many evil geniuses is that they've spent years perfecting their academic skills, but they rarely take time to brush up their social skills. And this inability to connect with others is usually the root of the evil genius's social failure and lack of power.

We've all seen movies about, and heard tales of, the mad

scientist who becomes an outcast of society, then goes into his secret lab and creates monsters, and does other horrific deeds. This isn't too far from reality, because some of the most infamous serial killers have been diagnosed as being very intelligent men who were socially powerless.

Many postal workers are men who have a great amount of responsibility, but feel no sense of power. These guys have a lot of duties to fulfill, and the pay is subpar. And because of the strenuous drug testing that is done on postal employees, these guys can't even hit the weed, or engage in too many other intoxicants after work to relieve some of their job stress. This is why so many postal workers eventually snap, and start shooting up their job.

These are just a few extreme examples of the evil geniuses. In not-so-extreme instances, where many intelligent, professional black men feel limited because of discrimination, they too feel a great sense of frustration. But these brothas know way too well the consequences of even *thinking* about doing anything illegal, so they vent their frustration in more subtle ways. These guys will engage in strange sexual habits, or live double lives by having a secret family in another city.

Intelligent men who are socially powerless are some of the biggest cheaters. When they feel they can't be a dominant force in society, they can always resort to dominating coochie.

The Pushover

The pushover brotha is an easygoing, nonconfrontational guy. These guys like to come across as being sensitive to a woman's needs. The pushover likes to do little sentimental and romantic things, like buy women flowers, and take them on expensive dates.

These men were taught at a young age to put women on a pedestal, and do things like open doors and place their coats over puddles for women. The problem with many pushover brothas is they don't know how to balance their sensitivity. They often come across as being too nice and not having any backbone. This turns many women off from the pushover brotha. There are four subcategories of the pushover:

The Mama's Boy

The mama's boy was usually raised in a single-parent household by a domineering mother figure who smothered and spoiled him. This type of nurturing has prevented him from living up to his fullest potential as a man, so when he dates, he looks for women to be his new surrogate mother.

The mama's boy gets into relationships where he lets the female call the shots and make all the decisions. And whenever there is a problem with his girlfriend or wife, or any other aspect of his life, he is quick to go running back home to his real mama.

The Ultra-Gentleman

The ultra-gentleman goes out of his way to play the "good black man" role in front of women. This is the kind of guy who will constantly brag about how he's not like other men, and he will pretend to despise guys who are players and macks. But in reality, he secretly wishes he could be one.

The ultra-gentleman will pretend to enjoy going on romantic dates with women, and he will play his "super Negro" role to the fullest. He will open doors, pull out chairs, and do all sorts of so-called gentlemanly things for women. That is, until he gets some ass.

Remember: The definition of a gentleman is a man who hasn't had sex with you yet.

The ultra-gentleman knows that women like men to give them special attention by being extra courteous. This is why the ultra-gentleman plays this role. The problem is, he plays this role with every woman he's trying to bang. So women shouldn't feel too flattered by this charade.

If you want to see a perfect example of the ultra-gentleman, watch any movie starring Morris Chestnut or Taye Diggs. These guys are famous for playing the super black man roles, and their portrayal of ultra-gentleman is so enticing because they are *acting*. The only difference between an ultra-gentleman and these actors is that Morris and Taye are acting onscreen, and the ultra-gentleman is acting in person. Once you let the ultra-gentleman hit it, you will see him turn into an ultra-asshole.

The Righteous Bohemian Brotha

Even though there are some bohemian brothas who are sincere with their lifestyle, the average boho brotha is just a guy who tries to impress women by coming across as being more spiritual and righteous than other guys. The boho brotha is the type of cat who might wear dreads or an afro. He prides himself on being anti-establishment and he often makes a couple of dollars by selling incense, oils, and sometimes weed.

The boho brotha like to drink herbal tea, and read poetry. And he often listens to music by artists like Maxwell, Musiq Soulchild, and The Roots. In the white community, these types of guys are commonly referred to as hippies.

Sure there are some bohemian brothas who are genuinely in touch with nature and their inner peace. But there are many boho brothas who use this lifestyle as an excuse to get high and be nonproductive.

Captain Save-a-Ho

The Captain Save-a-Ho brotha is the pushover who likes to come to a woman's rescue, in the hopes of winning her over for sex. These guys usually have no game whatsoever and they try to use money, gifts, and generous deeds as a way to indirectly control women.

These guys will offer to come by a woman's home to fix things, move furniture, do yard work, fix her car, and so on. They offer to pay women's rent, bills, car notes, and they love offering to take women shopping. These guys are basically big tricks, and they think the more gifts they buy for a woman, the better their chances will be to get some ass.

Like many other pushovers, Captain Save-a-Ho tries to play the "friend" role at first. If the female already has a boyfriend, Captain Save-a-Ho always claims that he can treat her better than her man can. He is quick to hate on real macks, and he is always willing to "save" women from "bad boys" who are no good for them.

He is always the guy who has a shoulder for a female to cry on, and if the female has kids, he will claim to want to do things for the kids in order to win brownie points from the female. He likes to make all types of promises to a female, knowing that all he wants to do is hit it. Captain Save-a-Ho will often paint the picture of a romantic future with a female. And because he is so willing to trick off a few dollars at a moment's notice, his promises sound very convincing.

Captain Save-a-Ho definitely knows how to come across as a superhero. But if he's Superman, his kryptonite is pussy. Because the minute you let him get some ass, he goes right back to being Clark Kent.

The Parolee

The parolee is the street cat who was brought up in, and influenced by, the hard-knock inner city environment. Though there are some parolees who are true to the game, and live by a code of honor, the majority of parolees could also be classified as scrubs (in the white community, these types of guys are commonly referred to as slackers).

Some parolee brothas use their inferior social condition as an incentive to educate themselves, get their paper together, and get up out of the 'hood. Other parolee brothas fully embrace ignorance and poverty, and make it part of their identity. There are four subcategories of the parolee brotha:

The True Hustler

The true hustler is the only category of parolee who is not considered a scrub. The true hustler is a real street cat whose primary focus is stacking his paper so he can stay out of jail and get out of the 'hood. The true hustler may have started out as a gangbanger, car thief, or any other type of low-level hustler, until he upgraded his street game to bigger and more lucrative hustles.

The true hustler may have been to jail a few times, but unlike a lot of other parolees who look at doing jail time as a badge of honor, he is hell-bent on not going back. The true hustler might engage in major drug deals, insurance scams, pimpin', or gambling

Even though many true hustlers are very well known in their neighborhoods, these guys have a pretty mellow demeanor, and they often try to keep a low profile. The public has always been infatuated with true hustlers. This stems from the Robin Hood era, where outlaws would steal from the rich and give to the poor. This infatuation is also evident with the popularity of infamous street hustlers and mob figures such as Bonnie and Clyde, Al Capone, Dillinger, Noriega, John Gotti, and Iceberg Slim. The reason so many people are intrigued with the true hustler is because these guys give off an air of excitement and adventure that both men and women desire to be a part of.

The Wannabe Thug

This type of parolee is very dangerous. The problem with the wannabe thug is that he *wishes* he could be a true hustler. Ninety percent of all wannabe thugs were raised by single mothers, so they have no realistic idea of what real manhood is. These guys have to overcompensate for their lack of knowledge of what being a man is by doing all types of senseless, shoot-'em-up shit, just so they can get a rep in their 'hood.

This is the kind of guy who likes to show out in public, walk around with a mean mug look on his face, and drink 40s and smoke blunts twenty-four/seven. The wannabe thug tries to convince people that he's tough, by always being down to fight or shoot if a person does something like look at him wrong, or steps on his shoe by mistake. Little does he know that this is a *feminine* reaction to a situation, because it's a response based on emotions.

These guys learned how to react emotionally to every situation by being raised by a number of women, with no male figure around to give them balance. See, it's OK for a female to have an emotional reaction to situations, because society gives women the cushion to do that. A woman can go out in the streets and talk shit to people and pretty much get away with it, because people know that she isn't going to hurt anybody. They know that she's just running her mouth. But a man can't get away with going out in the streets and just talking shit to people, because they know that he has the potential to cause them harm.

So, if a man is being confrontational because of an emotional reaction, he might get blasted on, because some people won't wait around to see if he is a potential threat. The wannabe thug is a perfect example of a rebel without a cause. The reason why there are so many wannabe thugs is because you can become a thug overnight. All a guy has to do is put some braids in his hair, let his pants sag, put on a wife-beater T-shirt, learn a few rap songs, and voila! He's an instant thug.

The 'Bout-To Brotha

The 'bout-to brotha is the parolee who is always bragging about what he's " 'bout to" do, but you never see him do it. He's always talking about he's " 'bout to" buy a new Lexus, he's " 'bout to" get a record deal, he's " 'bout to" get signed to the NBA, he's " 'bout to" buy a six-bedroom house, he's " 'bout to" open up a club.

The 'bout-to brotha might claim he's working as a barber until his album comes out, or that he's staying with his mama until he goes off to NFL training camp. The 'bout-to brotha is very insecure and has no confidence in himself, so he creates a fantasy world, and tries to lure others into it.

Instead of trying to achieve real goals, this parolee is totally content with just trying to convince people that he is about to achieve greatness. There is an old saying that *doers never talk, and talkers never do.* Most women who have themselves together know better than to fall for the 'bout-to brotha's bullshit. And the women who do fall for the 'bout-to brotha's game are usually superficial women who are impressed by his false credentials.

Sure, it's shallow for a man to go around lying to women, telling them that he's " 'bout to" get signed to the Lakers, or he's " 'bout to" get an Escalade. But if a woman is shallow enough to sleep with a man because she thinks he's an NBA player or that he drives an expensive car, the two of them are a perfect match and they each deserve what they get.

The Professional Baby Daddy

The professional baby daddy is on the very bottom of the parolee totem pole. His low-level hustle is to have children by a number of different women, so he can then live off them. Many men feel they can always have security with women who have their children. And the professional baby daddy milks this for all it's worth.

This parolee is extremely irresponsible and immature, and when he's around his kids and baby mothers he acts more like one of the kids than a father. This guy has no integrity and no respect for the game or anything whatsoever.

Since he has nothing else going on for him in life, he can only think in terms of survival. Like the cavemen I mentioned earlier, he has reverted to his primal instincts to just procreate. The majority of women he has children by are chickenheads (who else would allow themselves to have children by this guy?), and he knows that when these women get pregnant and have his kids, they will immediately get on Section 8, or any other type of government assistance—thus insuring that he will always have a place to stay and a place to eat.

The professional baby daddy loves to play his baby mothers against each other. And having a bunch of chickenheads fighting over him gives this low-expectations brotha a tremendous ego boost. He doesn't worry about any of his baby mothers becoming vindictive toward him and trying to file for child support. He knows (and the mothers know) it's pointless, because they can't garnish his wages. The professional baby daddy doesn't have a job! So in his mind, he has nothing to lose and everything to gain by having a number of baby mammas.

Ladies, if you meet a guy who has three or more kids by three different women, then more than likely you are dealing with a professional baby daddy.

Now that you have a general understanding of the different types of men that are out on the dating scene, I must also point out that there are "combination brothas." There are some players with parolee characteristics, and there are some pushovers with professional traits.

There are also a few more personality traits that women should look for in men. Now the next four personality traits can be found in any one of the four Ps, and these guys are very common out on the dating scene:

Other Personality Traits

The Sassy Brotha

When people hear the term "sassy brotha," they automatically think that this has homosexual implications. But the sassy brotha isn't gay whatsoever. He's just a guy who overly accentuates his wardrobe. The sassy brotha is like the male version of a hoochie. This is the type of guy who wears see-through shirts, tight leather jeans with sandals and a toe ring, or a V-necked sweater with a choker.

The sassy brotha is the guy who likes to wear his shirt unbuttoned at the bottom so he can show his abs and his belly ring. Some sassy brothas will go so far as to get their eyebrows arched and their tongues pierced. Guys like Shemar Moore, Eric Benet, Lenny Kravits, and Johnny Gill are perfect examples of sassy brothas.

Many women are instinctively skeptical about investing too much into a relationship with a sassy brotha. Like I mentioned before, women instinctively look for leadership and protective skills in a man. And how can a man protect his woman and family from the dangers of the world if he's wearing a fur vest with no shirt under it, a nipple ring, some flip-flops, and an ankle bracelet?

The Pretty Boy

This guy is vain and stuck on himself. He knows that men focus primarily on physical attributes of women, and he thinks women are just as concerned with the way a man looks. So the pretty boy spends 95 percent of his time making sure his looks are in order.

It's virtually impossible for the pretty boy to *not* look at his reflection. This guy is constantly in the mirror, and if he walks by a parked car, he has to look at his reflection in the side mirror.

The pretty boy spends a lot of time working out in the gym, and whatever hairstyle he has, you can bet that it will be hella moist. Since he doesn't focus on anything else besides his physical being, he doesn't even attempt to elevate himself or expand his mind. This is why many pretty boys are plain ignorant.

Many women can attest to having an encounter with a man they thought was extremely attractive at first, but once they got to know his personality, he didn't seem that attractive anymore.

The Super Scrub

The super scrub is the brotha who can never seem to fully get his shit together. Just like the rest of society, the super scrub has the potential to be successful, but he has become comfortable with being an underachiever.

If the super scrub is doing something that he might become successful in, he will subconsciously self-sabotage his own efforts. He does this because if he were to show his full capabilities, people would expect more from him on a continuous basis. This means he would have to be more responsible. And the super scrub is terrified of responsibility.

The super scrub is another guy who didn't grow up with a father figure, and he often uses the emotional logic passed down from his mother. And as I mentioned earlier, *emotional* logic for men still leads to *real* results. This is why the majority of super scrubs are parolees.

Many super scrubs have what I call the "Kunta Kinte" mentality. They blame everything wrong in their lives on "the white man" and racism. The super scrub will often say things like, "Why should I even try getting a job, the white man isn't going to hire me," or "I'm staying with my mama, because they won't let a black man like me move into a plush apartment."

Now, of course, we can't ignore the fact that racism plays a dominant role in the daily lives of black men in America. But what raises a black man to a king's status is how he works *around* prejudice, and becomes successful in spite of racism instead of accepting failure because of racism.

Even if the super scrub was given an equal opportunity, or even some sort of advance financial incentive to use toward upgrading himself, he still wouldn't take full advantage of it. The super scrub has a scrub mentality. You could give him $50,000 to start a business or to get his life in order, and he would spend $40,000 on a new Navigator, and the other $10,000 on a watch and chain. He would rather *look* successful than *be* successful.

The super scrub has plenty of idle time to hang out and kick it. His favorite pastime is to sit around the house (usually with other scrubs) and play X-Box or Sega Genesis, smoke blunts, and chase chickenheads. Surprisingly, there are a lot of women who are attracted to super scrubs (especially the parolee types) because they find something intriguing about a man who's rough around the edges. Plus, women like the fact that these guys know how to hit that ass right, and that is pretty much the only trump card the super scrub has.

Men deal with chickenheads and hoochies because in many cases these women know how to throw the coochie better. These women have had a lot of practice having sex, starting at a young age. And when they get older, adventurous sex is all a chickenhead or hoochie can bring to the table, when it comes to dating. And men don't require anything more from them. A man will seldom try to change a chickenhead or try to turn a hoochie into something that she's not.

Women like scrubs for the same sexual reasons. Many women know that super scrubs can throw the dick better than the average guy. But because there is such a negative stigma in our society toward women who have uncommitted sex, women have to find reasons to justify having sex with scrubs. So, they will go out of their way to try and find something salvageable about the super scrub's personality. This is like trying to find treasure in a trash can. This is also why many women will find themselves dating a man based on his potential rather than his credentials.

Women look at these guys as being diamonds in the rough. And these women think that all these scrubs need to get is a little polishing, and then they can *truly* shine. Well, ladies, the truth is (as you should know) you can't change any man. All you can do is accept him for what he really is. And if he's a scrub, don't try to bullshit yourself into believing that he is anything different.

Here's a quick reference list that will give you some clues on the personality of a super scrub.

Top five ways to tell if a man is a super scrub:

1. He rents expensive cars so he can park in front of the club when it's over.

2. He has to take the bus to make booty calls.

3. He works at IBM and sells weed on the side.

4. He's a grown man, but he still talks about playing video games as if he's partaking in a real event.

5. His main priority is to save money so he can buy rims for his car.

Tricks

Tricks are men who have such a deficiency in their game that they feel they have to just straight-up pay for sex. Trickin' is like being in a competition, throwing in the towel, and just buying the trophy. So for a man to trick means that he is admitting to himself that he is a failure. He is saying that he has no game whatsoever, and he cannot get a female based on his own character.

There are many men who have trick tendencies. And there are men who are just blatant tricks. And the blatant tricks are the ones you need to watch out for.

Many tricks were taught at a young age that a man is supposed to place a woman on a pedestal. But they were erroneously taught that women should be on a pedestal simply because they are females. So in essence, they were taught that a person should be worshipped and respected more if they have a vagina (when they should have been taught to give people respect and praise based on their *character*). This type of teaching programmed these men into believing that the vagina has value. So these men will offer other things of value (such as money, cars, jewelry) in exchange for the vagina.

Dealing with tricks is a catch-22 situation. On the one hand, since tricks are motivated by the hope of getting a female's vagina, the female can use her vagina as a bargaining chip to get attention, gifts, and money. But on the other hand, a women can use her vagina to control and manipulate the trick at her disposal. And no matter how much women hate to admit it, no woman wants a man she can control, which is why many women lose respect for tricks.

The Type of Men That Women Generally Find Appealing

The kind of men women *want* and the kind of men women *need* at the moment are two different things. When people perceive shortcomings in their own lives, they will subconsciously seek out companions who can compensate for what they lack.

A woman on the dating scene might *want* a parolee brotha, because she is sexually turned on by that roughneck image. But if she is in debt, has bills due, and her lights are about to be turned off, it's only natural for her to gravitate toward a potential pushover or a trick. Let's face it, ladies, if you have bills due, you can't go down to your local power company and tell them "I can't pay the bill this month, but I got some good dick at home." You and that good dick will be sitting in the dark.

So the type of men that women go for depends on the type of advantages or deficiencies the woman feels she has in her life. (We will work on rectifying some of these deficiencies in other chapters.) This will often cause a woman to compromise what kind of man she *wants* for a man she will just *accept.*

Men think like this as well. I don't think that there is a man on this planet who wouldn't get with Halle Berry, because she is generally considered to be one of the finest women in the world. Now the average man might *want* and fanatisize about having a female who is as fly as Halle, but he may have to *accept* a female who is not as fine as she is. And a woman might *want* a brother like Denzel Washington, but she might have to accept a brother of a lesser caliber.

But if the average man could get with a Halle Berry type, he *would* get with her. And if the average female could get with a Denzel, she *would* get with a Denzel.

Women and men pretty much share general criteria when it comes to the opposite sex (we will get into the men's criteria a little later). Women generally want what I like to call the urban Renaissance man. The urban Renaissance man is basically a combination of all the positive aspects of the four Ps: smooth and sexy like the player, intelligent and financially stable, like the professional, compassionate at times, like the pushover, and able to tap that ass real good, like the parolee.

Women are intrigued by Renaissance men like James Bond. Females like the 007 character, because he has the four Ps persona. Bond is very suave (like the player). He is very intelligent in the way he figures out how to get out of certain situations, and he has fly clothes and nice cars (like the professional). He can be gruffly sensitive (like the pushover). He lives a dangerous and adventurous life, and he knows how to put it down with the ladies (like the parolee).

The late rapper Tupac Shakur was a modern Renaissance man because he was so universally appealing. Tupac showed his player side with songs like "I Get Around" and "Toss It Up." He showed his professional side whenever he did interviews, and many of the people who knew him personally would attest to how intelligent he was. He showed his pushover side with songs like "Brenda's Got a Baby" and "Dear Mama." And of course we all got to see his thug side.

Denzel Washington is one of the few actors who can successfully pull off portraying any one of the four Ps, making him irresistible to women. Denzel is so universally admired by females, because he can portray the player (like he did in *Mo' Better Blues*), he can portray the professional (like he did in *Malcolm X*), he can portray the pushover (like he did in *John Q*), and he can play the parolee (like he did in *Training Day*).

So ladies, if you want to have a Renaissance man, you have to become a Renaissance woman. Even if you don't want a Renaissance man at the moment, you still need to become an urban Renaissance woman. Because an urban Renaissance woman has the credentials to get any one of the four Ps she may need for the moment.

Now that you have a general description of all the different types of men out there, it's time to understand why certain women will date certain types of guys. There are women who will read this chapter and still go out and date a scrub, and continue to complain that the relationship isn't working. So in this next chapter, we are going to break you *ladies* down, and focus on what makes you tick . . . Brace yourself.

Tip #3 on how women can have game:

Become a "nonverbal language" reader.

This will help you make sure a man's actions are always in correlation with his words. And you can peep this out when you first meet a man. If a man says he is going to call you at eight o'clock, and he calls you at eleven o'clock, you need to acknowledge that in your mental Rolodex. And if he has a number of little inconsistencies such as this, you need to acknowledge that this may be a red flag. Because in most cases, if a man is inconsistent about little things, he will be inconsistent about major things.

4: Are You a Hoochie? Take the Chickenhead Test

One of the main qualities that people request from the opposite sex is honesty. We all want somebody who is going to be real with us. Now ladies, you all know that there are some men out there who lie. There are some cats out there who lie their asses off (as if I had to tell you this). But the thing is, most men who lie *know* that they are full of shit.

You see, women lie too (let's keep it real, ladies). And women's lies are more effective because women lie to *themselves*. This causes many women to believe their own bullshit. Women lie to themselves about a lot of things, not just relationships. There are women who weigh over three hundred pounds, and swear they can wear a size six. These women will squeeze into an outfit that is way too small, and swear they look good in it. There are women who wear hair weaves for so long, they start to believe that it's their real hair, and will get offended if you imply that it's a weave.

No matter how much you fantasize or live in self-denial, how the world is going to treat you will be based on the reality of your actions. A woman may be a full-fledged chickenhead, but in her own mind, she is classy. However, the men she deals with are still going to step to her on a chickenhead level. And these women will go through life not having the slightest clue why their relationships aren't turning out the way they want them to.

This is why it is extremely important for females to be completely honest with themselves about the type of women they really are. When you are honest about who you are, you will have a better understanding of why you attract the men that you do.

Now I know that a major pet peeve of many women is being categorized. Women hate to be put in the same category as other women. They will go out of their way to *appear* to be different or unique. Since a woman's basic primal instinct is to get attention, individuality is almost a survival trait.

Most men who have themselves together want a female to be unique. These men *want* women who stand out from the crowd in a positive way. The reality is, many women aren't as unique as they think they are. These women might come across as being unique to guys who are new to the game. But when these women encounter a seasoned player, who has dealt with a number of women, they aren't saying or doing anything that he hasn't seen and heard a million times before. This type of guy has a "player's Rolodex" that he can always refer back to when he deals with females. So he already knows how to react to a female in order to satisfy his own agenda.

So ladies, this is why it is important to change your game up. And before you change or upgrade your game, you need to have an understanding of where you are now, game-wise.

How Men Really Judge Women

Let's face it, the way a woman looks is always a pertinent issue in our society. But women focus on the way they and other women look *way* more than men do (L'Oréal cosmetics isn't a multibillion-dollar corporation for nothing). Women uphold and enforce the standard of beauty in society more than men, because women are more judgmental of other women's looks.

If a female singer or actress is in a video or on an award show with one hair out of place, other women will pick her apart. Men don't care if Toni Braxton's dress don't match her shoes.

In our society, women are judged by their looks and how their game is in accordance with one another. As I mentioned before, the street definition of game means having intelligence, hustle, and common sense.

You are about to get a true understanding of how men *really* look at women. Men place women into one of five basic game/attractiveness categories. This will determine what class the female will be in. There are:

1. A-class females
   (attractive women with game)

2. B-class females
   (attractive women with no game)

3. C-class females
   (mannequins)

4. D-class females
   (unattractive women with game)

5. F-class females
   (unattractive women with no game)

A-Class Females
(Attractive women with game)

The A-class female, also known as the top-notch female, is the lady that other women aspire to be. The A-class females are the Halle Berrys, the Janet Jacksons, and the Tyra Bankses of the world.

They are very attractive women who have a lot of game to back up their looks. They are the most successful of all the classes of women, and this is why they can choose from a better selection of men at their disposal.

The most admirable thing about the A-class female is that she could have easily relied strictly on her beauty to get whatever she wanted out of life, but she chose to make that extra effort to upgrade her game. This is what makes her the shit.

The A-class female is an urban Renaissance woman. She's attractive. Physically fit. Very well educated. She has a little street flavor, but she's far from ghetto. She's very intelligent, but she's not corny. She's strong willed, but she maintains her femininity, and she is still sexy. And sexiness is the key ingredient to being a top-notch, A-class female.

Some lesser females feel that once they have achieved a certain level of academic or financial success, they have to harden their demeanor in order to maintain that success. They start making over $12 an hour, and suddenly they start walking around like they are Xena, the Warrior Princess. But the A-class female doesn't compromise her sexiness in exchange for her success.

B-Class Females
(attractive women with no game)

The B-class female is an attractive female who relies solely on her looks to get by in life. The B-class female will usually get the basic necessities out of life. She can get guys to buy her food. She can get guys to take her to the mall to get clothes. She can get guys to pay her bills. But the B-class female rarely comes up big time.

Many B-class females are attention freaks, and their whole existence revolves around attracting a successful man so that he might "save" her. The B-class female can easily get a man, but she has a hard time keeping a man.

And because they have no game to back up their looks, many B-class females aspire to be actresses or models, because they think that all they have to do is look cute, and people will pay them for it. They don't understand that great actresses still have to work hard by going to drama and dialect classes to succeed. And professional models have to be disciplined and stick to a strict diet regimen in order to stay fit. The B-class female is too lazy to do all of that, and this laziness is the reason why many B-class females only rise to a groupie or stripper status.

An attractive female who has had the world given to her on a silver platter really has no incentive to acquire any other type of knowledge or higher learning. Sure, she might take a few "decoy classes" in school, to appear that she is trying to get a career crackin' off. But she is really waiting for Prince Charming to come along.

The fairy tale of Cinderella taps into a basic desire that most women have of: *"No matter how broke I am, if I look good enough, long enough, a rich man will come and rescue me."*

And the B-class female embodies the Cinderella syndrome to the fullest. She might live in humble surroundings (the 'hood), with her "evil stepsisters" (other women in the 'hood who are envious of her looks). She will save just enough money to get a few fly outfits and shoes (glass slippers), she will get made up so she can go to the royal ball (the nightclub), and hopefully she will convince "Prince Charming" (a baller) that she really has it goin' on.

The reality is, the B-class female lives in a constant state of insecurity. Just like Cinderella, she knows that her whole persona is smoke and mirrors. So she has to hurry up and find Prince Charming by "midnight."

Of course, for the B-class female, "midnight" is usually twelve o'clock the next afternoon, because that's when she has to take the clothes with the tags still on them back to the mall. Then she has to return the rented Lexus (the carriage), and drive her bucket (the pumpkin) right back to the 'hood.

B-class females know that their looks are the only thing they have going for them, and because of this they live in a state of insecurity. However, at the same time, they have become comfortable with having everything given to them, and this causes them to have a lazy mentality.

It's hard for a woman to get out of a comfort zone when she is still getting her basic needs (and primal desire for attention) taken care of. But these women know that when those looks go (which they will) it's all over for them.

C-Class Females
(Mannequins)

The mannequin is the female who has a look that will be enhanced or reduced, based on her persona. She's not drop-dead gorgeous, but she isn't a mud duck either. A C-class female might look average at first glance, but if she has a sexy attitude or a cool disposition, that could elevate her from being a 5 to an 8.

And there are some C-class females who look kind of cute at first glance, but then they open their mouths and start spittin' some ghetto nonsense, and just mess up their whole vibe. So the C-class female's game has a direct impact on the way people view her beauty.

A bad attitude makes a C-class female appear unattractive. It's no different from a female meeting an attractive guy who, at first glance, makes you want to jump his bones. And then you get to know him, and you find out he's a dumb ass. This turnoff is no different from when kings (not cavemen, because they will deal with anything with a vagina) are checking out a potential mate.

D-Class Females
(Unattractive women with game)

The D-class female doesn't necessarily have to be unattractive, but she is the female who has known from an early age that she is not going to get over in life strictly based on her physical attributes. So she has learned to hone in on another skill or talent.

The D-class female usually becomes an overachiever in many of her endeavors. She might become a very gifted student. She might become very gifted in sports. She might become very knowledgeable in the business or political world.

Women like Oprah, Janet Reno, Whoopie Goldberg, Venus and Serena Williams, Gloria Alred, and Star Jones all became very successful in their respective fields because they knew that looks alone weren't going to cut it for them (and some of these women actually began to look a little better after they got a little paper).

Some D-class females will try to criticize A- and B-class females for using their looks as a stepping-stone to reach certain achievements. The D-class female will often try to come across like she's taking the moral high road by not having to rely on physical attributes, when in reality, she *can't* rely solely on physical attributes. Many D-class females will proclaim things like "I'm independent and I pay my own bills," or "I don't *let* guys do anything for me." But the reality is they usually have no choice but to pay their own rent and bills. Because if they didn't, they would starve.

For the most part, if a guy does have major league money to trick off on a female, he's going to do it on an A- or B-class female.

F-Class Females
(unattractive women with no game)

These females are the bottom-feeders of the game. Just like their male scrub counterparts, there are more F-class females than any other female. These are the chickenheads. These are the hoodrats. And many of these women are hoochies.

In the Caucasian community, these women are commonly referred to as trailer trash (or white trash). These are women who don't have the looks to come up, and are too lazy to educate themselves and learn some game. This is why the majority of them live lives of poverty.

If you go to any housing project, welfare building, trailer park, or swap meet, the majority of people you will see are unattractive women with no game.

There are more F-class females than any other class of female because it's easy to be a chickenhead. All you have to do is be nonproductive and blame everyone else for your misfortunes. Because the F-class female has no looks or no skills (by her own choice) to be appreciated for, she becomes desperate for attention, and will do anything for it. This is why you see chickenheads with the ghetto hairstyles, long flamboyant fake fingernails, loud hoochie clothes, a dozen tattoos, and huge gaudy jewelry.

These women will do anything it takes to bring attention to themselves. If you are in a public place, and you hear a group of people acting loud and obnoxious, most likely it's a bunch of F-class females. These women can be at an upscale restaurant, and they will still laugh, talk loud, and cackle at the top of their lungs in order to bring attention to themselves.

F-class females are usually nonproductive, so they generally have a lot of idle time on their hands. And they utilize this idle time by keeping up a bunch of petty, gossipy nonsense in their communities.

These are the women you see on court TV shows, suing each other for $70 because one of them didn't put the other one's weave in right. One of the most common ways we men can spot a potential chickenhead is by her name. Many chickenheads have first names that end with the syllable "esha." When men hear names like "Shaquesha," "Kalesha," or "Lacresha," we already have an idea of what 'hood she is from.

I think one of the reasons that ghetto names have become so popular over the years is because of the epidemic of teen mothers in this country. These young girls are having babies, and they are too immature to give their children names that will properly represent them in the future. When I meet a twenty-one-year-old female with a name like "Donquesha," I can almost guarantee that she has a mother who is in her mid-thirties, because this is a product of teen parenthood.

Many of these teen mothers are so concerned with giving their children a name that nobody else has, they don't know how to draw the line between *unique* and *absurd.* I have friends who are schoolteachers in urban areas, and they tell me that children today have names so ghetto, it's becoming almost impossible to pronounce them.

In a chickenhead's mind, any name with a "La," "Sha," or "Q" in it sounds French. And to them, names that have French sounds in them are supposed to sound *sophisticated.*

I'm going to speak on behalf of the children, because they can't speak for themselves:

Ladies, from this point on, *stop naming your kids ghetto names.* It's not cute. It's not unique. It's not original. All you are doing is placing a stigma on your children, and creating unnecessary obstacles for them in the future.

Now I know that people *shouldn't* be judged by their names. I know that people *should* be judged based on their character, but first impressions are often lasting ones. And in many cases, people's names will automatically give you an impression of what they might be like. When you hear a name like "Billy Bob," you think of a hillbilly or a redneck. When you hear a name like "Raheim," you think of a young black man from the East Coast, who is into hip-hop. When you hear a name like "Megan," you think of a white girl from the suburbs. And when you hear a name like "BaQueba," what image pops into your head? That's right, *hoodrat.* So, as a reminder, ladies, those ghetto names are only considered cute by other chickenheads.

The major problem with chickenheads is that they don't know that they are chickenheads. Most F-class females don't have any other references outside of the 'hood to compare from. In their world, their behavior is considered normal. So

I've compiled a test of twenty ways to tell if you might be a chickenhead.

Now many non-chickenheads may have a couple of chickenhead *tendencies*. But if four or more items on the test apply to you then I'm afraid that you are a certified, full-fledged chickenhead.

Top twenty ways to tell if you might be a chickenhead:

1. If you wear animal prints from more than one animal at a time.

2. If your weave doesn't match your real hair.

3. If you date guys for food.

4. If you wear acrylics on your toenails.

5. If your car note is more than your rent.

6. If you wear eyeliner pencil around your lips.

7. If you wear purple braids.

8. If you are eight months pregnant and still going to clubs.

9. If you keep empty liquor bottles as souvenirs.

10. If you constantly have to put cocoa butter on your neck and forehead because you keep burning yourself trying to do your own hair.

11. If you drink a cup of soda, then chew the ice.

12. If techniques on how to commit welfare fraud have been passed down in your family from generation to generation.

13. If you talk about soap opera characters as if they were real people.

14. If you tried to rent a time-share in the Bahamas using your Section 8.

15. If you and your homegirls ever jumped somebody at a club.

16. If you have been living in an apartment for three months and you still sleep on a pallet.

17. If you go to Church's Chicken and order a hot pepper by itself.

18. If you have ever claimed your homegirls' kids as dependents so you can get more money from the county.

19. If you get tattoos to cover up stretch marks.

20. If you went to your prom in an Oldsmobile Cutlass.

Other Personality Traits That Men Peep Out

Now that I have listed the categories that men put women into, I want to point out some other personality traits that men see in women. This will give you ladies an idea of how certain men react to these types of women. These three types of females could be in any one of the class types, and they are very common on the dating scene.

The Overly Trendy Chick

There is nothing wrong with being up on the latest trends and wearing name brand clothes, but the overly trendy chick goes a little overboard. She is the female who sits up and watches BET all day, then tries to dress exactly like the females in the videos.

Now there's a difference between a hoochie and a trendy chick. A hoochie wears too little. But a trendy chic wears too much. And too many accessories will ruin an outfit. When a king sees a woman out at the club wearing low-cut jeans, cut-off shirt, a scarf wrapped around her waist, knee-high pointed boots and a big ass hat and shades, they look at her as trying too hard. She comes across as an attention freak.

Plus, when a female is too trendy, it makes her look like she is the kind of woman who is influenced by peer pressure. And men like a woman who can think for herself and not be influenced by her peers or the latest trends.

Men look at overly trendy chicks as being unstable, and men are not going to seriously invest in an unstable foundation. The funny thing about many overly trendy chicks, is that most don't need all that stuff. I have often seen very attractive women throw their whole look off track by trying to become a replica of the latest female singer or rapper that's on the charts at the moment.

If a woman is trying too hard to look like Alicia Keyes or Foxy Brown, the message she sends is that she's not comfortable with being herself. And if you don't like yourself, why should others like you?

The Cute Lil' Dingy Girl

A lot of women (especially B-class females) like playing the cute lil' dingy girl role, because some men like women who come across as being innocent and naïve. Being dingy also gives off the impression of being submissive, and these females know that a submissive woman is very gratifying to the male ego.

Now, for some women, this is not an act. Some cute women are *genuinely* dingy. These women feel that they don't have an incentive to become intelligent because they can be naïve, and still get the world handed to them on a silver platter. As a matter of fact, to them, being intelligent might throw a wrench in their program. Because if they began to show signs of intellect, other people might start expecting more from them. And the cute lil' dingy girl always has to come across as being the damsel in distress in order to have men come to her rescue.

There is nothing wrong with playing the dingy role, and trying to make a quick come up, as long as *you* know you are putting on an act. In many cases, when a woman is running game on other people, she ends up running game on herself. You can't live a cute lil' dingy girl lifestyle. The women who don't know they are dingy usually end up with a rude awakening, because they never upgrade their game.

The dingy routine only works for so long. And the only reason men even tolerate the cute lil' dingy' girl personality is because they ultimately just want to hit the ass. When a woman is young, the dingy role can work for her. But when she reaches a certain age, it's not cute anymore. When a woman is twenty-one and dingy, people can refer to her as the "cute lil' dingy girl." But when a woman is *forty-one* and dingy, people refer to her as "that old crazy bitch." Just take a look at the *Anna Nicole Show.*

The Boho Sista

The boho sista is the female equivalent to the boho brotha. She is the natural, earthy female, who is into herbal tea and incense. She wears her hair in braids, dreads, afros, or cut very short, and is adamant about not putting chemicals in her hair.

The boho female is often into poetry, and you will always find artists like Erika Badu, Jill Scott, or India.Arie in her CD collection. Many boho sistas are appealing because they have a very spiritual and nurturing demeanor. But on the flip side, some females get into the whole urban hippie vibe just so they can justify smoking weed and being counterproductive.

OK, ladies, by now you should have a good understanding of the different types of men, and you should have a pretty clear idea of the type of woman *you* are. Next, we are going to get into why certain types of women date certain types of men.

Tip #4 on how women can have game:

Realize that in most cases, you can control your looks.

Cosmetic tycoon Helena Rubenstein once said that "there are no ugly women, just lazy women." And this statement has a lot of truth to it. Physical attractiveness is usually altered by laziness and bad eating habits. Many women have issues and insecurities about their weight. And many women try to come up with all kinds of excuses as to why they have weight issues. But weight loss and weight gain all boil down to simple mathematics. If you consume X amount of food, without burning X number of calories, you will maintain X amount of weight. It's that simple. You just have to exercise and eat right. Don't blame your weight issues on genetics, diabetes, or giving birth to children. Anyone can control their weight if they really want to. If you notice, news footage during wartime never shows any fat hostages. That's because hostages are usually deprived of food. I guarantee you that if you get a woman like Star Jones, and put her in one of those Taliban prison camps for about three months, she will come back looking like Ashanti.

5: Common Mistakes
Women Make

In order to rectify any relationship problems you may have, you must first acknowledge that there is a problem. Nowadays, many women are reluctant to acknowledge any discrepancies they may have, because they don't want to give the impression of being weak or vulnerable. So this causes many women to put on their game face when dealing with relationship issues.

Pretending that all is well with your relationships issues is cool when you are trying to front for your peers, but you still have to be honest with *yourself*.

We are now going to examine the common mistakes that women make, and the different ways to rectify these mistakes.

Mistake # 1
Dating men based on your own expectations, instead of the reality he presents

A few years ago, I was watching a TV special called "When Animals Attack." The show featured a huge bear from a European circus. The bear's trainer had taught the animal to do all types of tricks and stunts.

This bear was trained to walk on his hind legs, ride bikes, dribble balls, and do flips. He got so good at these stunts that people started to feel very comfortable around him, and treated him as if he were Winnie the Pooh.

So the bear and its trainer were brought out in front of the cameras and the female host began to interview the trainer. Now the thing about some wild animals is, if you show them your teeth, they will take this as a sign of aggression. And they will instinctively interpret this as a challenge.

So the show host sits right next to the bear, and she's grinning from *ear to ear*. The bear happens to look over at her, sees her grinning, and the bear snaps. His natural instincts take over because now he thinks the woman is challenging him. All of a sudden, the bear starts attacking the woman. I mean, this bear tore this lady's ass up. They finally subdued the bear, and got the woman to safety.

After the bear attack, the "experts" all got together to try and figure out *what went wrong*. My answer to them is *nothing* went wrong. You know why I say that? Because *it's a bear*. Bears are *supposed* to tear your ass up if you mess with them. And because this bear was so well trained, the people around him became too comfortable, and forgot that he was still a vicious animal.

Many women get into this Trained Bear syndrome when dealing with men. You will be in a relationship with a guy, and you *knew* he was a scrub when you first met him. You *knew* he didn't have a job when you met him. You *knew* he was living at his mama's house when you met him. You *knew* he didn't have a car when you met him. You *knew* he was banging every chickenhead in the 'hood when you met him.

Then you got a hold of him, and you trained him to act the way you wanted him to act. You encouraged him to get a job. You let him stay at *your* crib. You let him use *your* car. You got him out of his natural habitat, and moved him into your "training camp." And the first few months, he acted the way *you* wanted him to. You trained him well.

But the minute your trained little poo-bear gets a taste of his natural habitat, by hanging out with one of his old homies, or hanging back out at the club where you met him, he goes right back to being a vicious grizzly.

And when he starts coming home with phone numbers, or coming home late (if at all), his woman has the nerve to act surprised and then whine how, "I don't know what went wrong." Nothing went wrong. He was that way when you first met him, and you *knew* he was that way.

The most common excuse women use when a man does show his true colors is "he wasn't like that in the beginning." But the reality is, these women don't see a man's true colors in the beginning, because they don't *want* to see his true colors in the beginning. Many women *choose* to ignore a man's true colors. But women have a very accurate emotional Rolodex, and they remember a man's early relationship discrepancies, and store them subconsciously into that Rolodex.

Women will acknowledge, in great detail, what they knew

from the beginning of the relationship. Women will say things like "I knew when I paged you that Monday, two years and three months ago, and you didn't call back until forty-five minutes later, that you were with your ex-girlfriend then, but I just didn't say nothing." Or women will say things like, "I knew when I met you a year ago, and you said you weren't working because you just signed a record deal, that you were full of shit."

So using the "he changed" excuse is played out, ladies. This brings us to:

Play or Be Played Rule #3

When a man's nonverbal language tells you what he's about, you better accept it.

Here are three simple ways to read a man's nonverbal language to see if he is really feeling you:

1. He makes direct eye contact with you.

2. He uses elaborate hand gestures when he's talking to you (this shows that he is confident in what he's saying).

3. Everything he is saying to you can actually be verified.

And here are some examples of a man's nonverbal language that indicate he might be playing you:

1. He avoids direct eye contact, specifically by glancing off to his left (this implies deception).

2. He tries to overexplain something very simple.

3. He's talking to you and his arms are folded or
   his hands are in his pockets (this implies that
   he may be hiding something).

Casting Men in Your Own Personal Chick Flick

The reason why so many women tend to ignore the signs of a
man's true personality when they meet him is because they are
too preoccupied with projecting their own expectations of
what they want a man to be. Females will write their own
chick flicks in their minds, then go out looking for men to cast
in their "movie."

So instead of acknowledging these men for who they are,
many women will try to find a way to work him into the script,
and when it comes to getting some poon-tang, men are great
actors. Notice I said that men are great *actors,* not to be mis-
taken with being great *liars.* A liar generally makes up stuff on
his own. But an actor recites the lines that are given to him.
And women in this situation are feeding the men their lines to
use for running game on them.

When a woman is out with a new man, and she says things
like "The problem with my last boyfriend is that he never
opened doors, or pulled out my chair for me," the nonverbal
message or "script" she is relaying to the new man is, "If you
want to earn points with me, you need to open doors, and pull
out my chair."

And if the new man wants to win the "part" in the movie,
he will act accordingly.

Men can only act or play the role for so long. Just like any
actor, a man will play the role required of him very convinc-
ingly until he wins his Academy Award (which is, in most
cases, some ass). After he wins his Oscar, he can get out of
character, and go back to being himself.

Mistake #2
Being in denial

Being in denial is, hands down, the biggest mistake women make when dealing with relationship issues. Society gives women more of a cushion to live in denial than it does men. Males are generally forced (oftentimes by the law) to deal immediately with the consequences of their actions. Whereas women have temporary safe houses to live in denial about certain things.

Now I specified *temporary* safe houses, because eventually the consequences of women's actions do catch up with them. And when they do, oftentimes it's too late to recoup. Denial is like a cancer. You can ignore it for a while, and it might not cause you immediate pain. But if you keep on ignoring it, and the cancer continues to take over your body, it eventually becomes inoperable.

There are women out there who will get into dysfunctional relationships with different scrubs and lowlifes over and over again. And these women will be in denial as to why they continue to choose to be in relationships like this. They will sit by and blame everyone else for the choices they make, and when these women reach a certain age, it finally dawns on them that they never took the time to learn some game. Now they find themselves with severe relationship battle scars, a ton of emotional baggage, and in some cases, a number of kids by different scrubs. Their market value has hit rock bottom.

A woman with game knows how to be honest with herself when she sees that something she is doing in her relationship is wrong. She will do what it takes to immediately rectify the situation, even if it means enduring temporary pain, so she can continue to stay fly for decades to come.

The Need for Immediate Pleasure vs. Immediate Pain

It is natural for the human brain to try and block out or rectify what gives us immediate pain. People will do whatever it takes to avoid it.

This is one of the reasons why women use denial as a major defense mechanism when dealing with immediate pain. Being in denial often gives people immediate pleasure, and dealing with reality sometimes brings on immediate pain. So ladies, you have to make a choice. Do you: (a) want to get immediate pleasure, but suffer from long term-pain, or (b) withstand immediate pain, so that it will lead to long-term pleasure?

I look at dealing with reality and denial like trying to get into physical shape. Now, you can get *immediate pleasure* by eating a bunch of Twinkies and Cinnabuns. But the *long-term* effect is that you will become extremely overweight. Or you can go to the gym and lift weights and work out. Now working out and lifting weights regularly will give you immediate pain, but you will get *long-term pleasure* by seeing the physical results of having a nicer body.

A woman with a lot of debt and financial problems can get immediate pleasure by telling herself that, eventually, a Captain Save-a-Ho brotha is going to come along and help her pay off all her bills. Now she may get temporary pleasure by being in denial, but when the creditors come along and repossess her car, the long-term effects of not having any transport will kick in. So it would be better for her to deal with the immediate pain or discomfort of not spending her money frivolously at the mall and at the shoe store, and enjoy the benefits of long-term financial stability.

A woman might be in a relationship with a man for eight years, and she might get temporary pleasure by being in denial and telling herself that they are eventually going to get married. But she will end up just wasting a lot of years on something that isn't going to happen. In her mind, being in denial is better than the immediate pain of dealing with reality.

Because the reality is, she has to get out of her comfort zone, and maybe chill by herself so she can work on getting her stuff together. Then she will be able to attract a more suitable mate who sees eye to eye with her.

In many cases, people are so complacent with being in their comfort zone, they equate *temporary discomfort* with *pain*. Just because something is giving you comfort, doesn't mean it's good for you in the long run. A person might become extremely comfortable with lying in bed all day.

At one point or another, we have all lain in bed, and tried to think of any excuse imaginable to stay there. We've all said things like, "Damn, I don't feel like getting up" . . . "Maybe I can call in sick" . . . "I don't *really* need to take this class today anyway" . . . "Maybe I can tell my boss my dog was shot in a drive by" . . .

We have all sat in bed and thought of some far-fetched excuses to not get up and experience that discomfort. But most people will deal with that temporary discomfort, because they would rather have the long-term effects of being able to work and pay their bills.

So ladies, you should never run and hide off in the comfort zone that denial provides you with. Because no matter how much you are stuck in denial, the world still goes on. And you will still have to deal with the effects and consequences of the world around you.

Mistake #3
Trying to dominate your relationships

Women dominating their relationships is a big issue in our society, especially in the black community. There are three categories of relationship power structures:

1. Man-woman relationships

2. Father-daughter relationships

3. Mother-child relationships

Here's a rundown of all three categories.

Man-Woman Relationships

In this type of relationship, the man and the woman come together on an equal playing field. On every team, there has to be a captain. So the man plays his role as the leader, and the woman plays her role as the strong foundation of the relationship.

Contrary to a lot of the feminist teachings, male *leadership* isn't synonymous with female *oppression*. When a man has good leadership skills, and he sincerely values his woman's input and opinions, this brings balance to the relationship. And this is the ideal relationship for most men and women in our society.

Father-Daughter Relationships

Here, the man controls everything. This type of relationship usually involves a sugar daddy who is involved with a much younger, trophy female. The female is generally a B-class

female, or another class female who didn't grow up with a
father. These women grow up looking for that father figure in
the men they date.

Mother-Child Relationships

This is very common among black men and women. Here the
woman is basically running everything and calling the shots.
The type of men who usually get into this type of relationship
are mama's boys, scrubs, or pushover men who are very
passive.

The type of women who usually get into these relationships
are women from the inner city, women who were raised by single mothers, or women who grew up with a passive father figure. Women who were raised by single mothers in the inner
city were used to seeing their mothers put on the dominating
"I'm the boss," and "I don't need no man" routine. So these
women grew up thinking this is the natural order of relationships. It then baffles them as to why this type of mentality
never actually works in relationships.

These women subconsciously seek out relationships with
needy guys, or scrubs who are in need of a mother figure.
Oftentimes, when a woman sees that a man is going through
some trials and adversities, her maternal instincts will come
into play, and she will feel compelled to come to his rescue.
And many men will get into these relationships and take on a
child-like role.

But maternal instincts are based on emotions, and as I said
before, emotions are fickle. They change with the weather, and
a man cannot follow a person who is driven by emotions. A
woman might be in a mothering mood one day, and the next
day her attitude will be "I don't want to see no more kids for
the rest of the day." And if a grown man is in that child role,

and the woman isn't in her maternal mood, she is really going to have contempt for him.

There is nothing worse to a woman than going through some problems or difficulties, and having a grown ass man who is always up under her, and he can't do nothing to help her out.

Why Black Men Allow Themselves to Be Dominated

Both the man and the woman must share the blame for a relationship that has become unbalanced because the woman dominates the man. I blame the man for not upgrading his leaderships skills. Black male leadership has always been demonized in this country. Every black male leader of the last hundred years has been assassinated figuratively and/or literally. So in the minds of many black men, standing up for yourself and being a leader equates to criticism, imprisonment, or even death.

This fear causes many black men to hide behind their women for protection. When these men finally leave their mother's nest, they seek out relationships with women who will act as surrogate mothers.

Black men today are criticized for being afraid to stand up to women whenever they are challenged. What these men are really afraid of are the *consequences* of what will happen to them if they were to get on a woman's bad side. Today, if a man has a disagreement with his woman, he can go to jail at the drop of a hat. And it doesn't have to be a case of domestic violence. Just the *accusation* of domestic violence can get a brotha sent away. Women know that law enforcement is all too willing to come scoop a brotha up, and this is the trump card that many women dangle over men's heads. A woman can loud talk a man, shout at him, get in his face, belittle him, or even strike him, because she knows she has a whole judicial system to back her up.

Government and law enforcement have always used black women to get to black men. So brothas basically feel like they have two choices when faced with conflicts in these relationships. They can (1) bow down to the woman and play the submissive role, or (2) walk away from the relationship.

The men who leave don't walk away because they can't deal with the woman. They walk away because they can't deal with her backup (law enforcement). No one is going to walk into a battle knowing he will lose.

How a Woman's Maternal Instincts Conflict with Her Desire for Male Leadership

Let's face it ladies, you have different moods for different days. One day you're in a maternal mood, the next day you're in a rebellious mood. Two of the strongest instincts a woman has are the maternal need to nurture, and the desire for a man who is a leader. It is important for a woman to find a man who can thoroughly satisfy her primal need for male leadership. Because a man who is a strong leader can still maintain his position if his woman's other instincts or mood swings come into play.

But if a man is in a mother-child relationship, and the woman switches out of her *maternal* mood, and gets into a *rebellious* mood, the relationship is now in trouble. Because if a woman challenges a brotha's manhood, and he can't defend himself or rise to the challenge because he's afraid that she might put him out of the house, he loses. And now the respect she has for him is gone.

If the woman has a man who is a leader, though—one who is not dependent on her—he would not only stand up to her challenges and rebellions, he would also be able to thoroughly put her in check whenever she got out of pocket.

Should a Woman Be Put in Check?

I know a lot of you ladies out there are saying things like, "Ain't no man gonna check me," or "I wish a man would try to tell me what to do . . . I'll curse him out!" Save all the tough chick, sista girl stuff for Oprah. Because this is the real deal: many of you ladies *want* a man to stand up to you, and check you when you *know* you are out of line.

Many women will specifically test a man just to see if he is capable of putting them in check. Now when I say "put in check," I don't mean a man should hit his woman in the head with a beer bottle, just because she didn't wash out the bathtub. He can put her in check by not tolerating her disrespect.

It is in a woman's nature to sometimes challenge, or rebel against, male authority. I think women do this subconsciously to test a man to see if he's still capable of standing up for himself, and if he has the ability to be a protector.

The first story in the Bible is about a relationship in which the woman challenged the man's authority, and the consequences they suffered when he didn't check her and stand up to the challenge. When Adam told Eve, "Look, don't mess with that tree over there. We are not supposed to mess with it," Eve rebelled against his authority and did it anyway.

And instead of Adam putting Eve in check for going against his specific instructions, he let her talk *him* into eating from the tree when he knew it was wrong. And that just messed up the game from that point on. Even though Eve was the one who took the initiative to rebel against God and Adam's instructions, the Bible does not say that her involvement was the world's first sin.

The world's first sin was attributed to *Adam,* because he was supposed to be a leader, and it was his responsibility to represent his family unit. Instead, he let his woman lead him, and that messed up the whole order of the family unit.

Now ladies, I want you to really take heed to what I'm gonna kick to you. And I want you to etch this in your brain for the rest of your lives. If you fully comprehend this, it will help alleviate many relationship problems you may have. I don't care what the daytime talk shows tell you, I don't care what your mama told you, I don't care what the feminists told you—*women cannot lead men in relationships.*

Ladies, I know it's great to be empowered, and to dominate many other aspects of your life. But you can't dominate in your relationships with men. It goes against the very nature of man and woman.

In our society, we constantly hear women bragging about how "women are runnin' thangs," and "we don't need no man," and "we women have everything we want." Well, if women have all this goin' on, why are there so many women who are dissatisfied? I'll tell you why. Because women don't really want to be "runnin' thangs" in their relationships.

The Irony of the Dominant Female

Many women get into mother-child relationships because they feel if they can control the actions of the man, they can protect themselves from being hurt by him. But if a man is 100 percent dependent on a woman, she will lose 100 percent respect for him. And she will oftentimes kick him to the curb simply because she has the option to do so.

The average man whose woman is dependent upon him will kick that woman to the curb only if she deserves it. But ladies, you know—once you have lost respect for a brotha, you will find any little reason to kick him to the curb. You will walk in the house like, "You left the toilet seat up? Pack yo' shit and get out."

Every woman who has had a relationship with a dependent man has given him the "you can get out of my house" speech at one point or another. This is because no woman wants a man who will jump whenever she says so. And yet women will continue to go through this confusing, frustrating cycle, because they look for men they can dominate, and once they dominate them, the women lose respect for them.

And trust me, I also blame the guys for letting themselves get into these situations. I know a lot of you ladies are saying, "But there aren't a lot of real men out there." The real men *are* out there. Are there a lot of weak men out there? Sure. Are there a lot of immature men out there? Absolutely. Are there a lot of passive men out there who will let women run all over them? Of course, but the kings are out there as well.

And just like top-notch queens, these kingly men have to be sought out, because they are rare. Ladies, it's your job to upgrade your game, so you can have access to the men who are leaders.

When you get into a mother-child relationship, you are just settling. What you are saying to yourself is, "I don't think that I'm qualified to get with a man who is a powerful leader, so I will play it safe with a man that I think I can mold."

Ladies, you can mold children, but you can't mold men.

Tip #5 on how women can have game:

Learn to realize and accept when something isn't working for you.

If you are in a relationship or dating situation that you don't find fulfilling, know when to let it go. You can't beat a dead horse. Plus, holding on to an unfulfilling relationship will oftentimes limit you from getting into a better, more meaningful relationship. It's like trying to buy furniture for your home. You can't bring a brand new, beautiful living-room set into your home if you are still holding on to that raggedy-ass sofa that has sentimental value. You have to be willing to let some of the junk in your life go.

6: The Victim Hustle

Women are constantly bombarded with the notion that they are "victims." Now who are women *really* victims of, which sector of society is the real perpetrator? Women have been tricked into believing that they are constantly being gamed on by evil men in this country, and that the patriarchal element of society wants to keep women "oppressed." Contrary to all the melodramatic nonsense being spewed about the brothas, the reality is this, ladies: men are not all out to destroy you or to keep you oppressed. If you are dating an average guy, the worst thing he will do is have sex with you and not call, because the average guy is sexually motivated.

Many women would like to believe that men are impressed by their exquisite sense of fashion, their bubbly personalities, their witty sense of humor, and their intellectual conversation. But the reality is the average man (and I emphasize *average*) just wants to hit the ass before he wants to get to know a female for all her other traits, and women are generally aware of this on a subconscious level.

But oftentimes women repress this reality with delusional hopes and expectations, and they will do this because women hate the notion of being reduced to a booty call. You will rarely, if ever, hear a woman admit that she was just a man's booty call. Knowing that she had such a menial significance to a man is a hard blow to a woman's ego. This is why you will hear women use overly dramatic terminology when describing the validity of their relationships.

Instead of admitting that they had to get out of a relationship with a man who was only interested in sexual gratification, these women will use overly extreme terms like "He was emotionally abusive," or "He was a psychological terrorist." This is why women need to have game, because game will not allow women to wallow in self-pity and victimhood.

And telling women that men are the roots of all their problems causes women to misdiagnose their social symptoms. So what is the real basis for a lot of the frustration and victimization that women feel in our society? The root of the problem can be traced to three main things:

1. Media capitalism and commercialism

2. Agencies with a legal or political agenda

3. Misguided feminism

Ironically, these three entities are the main ones that claim to look out for the best interests of women. Let's break them down and analyze the *real* effects they have on women's issues.

Media Capitalism and Commercialism

(Television shows, magazines, videos, and commercials)

Major media corporations are, first and foremost, businesses for profit. They understand that women are major consumers, but they also realize that women are "emotional spenders." And one of the most pervasive rules of business is that "the customer is always right." Since women are their most reliable customers, these media outlets have a vested interest in telling women that everything they do in life, no matter how nonproductive or even destructive it may be, is perfectly fine. If you look at daytime television, especially talk shows, you see that they are very careful not to offend or even criticize the female viewing audience. And they always keep the underlying front of "empowering" women. But if you take a *good* look at daytime television, are they really trying to empower you ladies?

Check out some of the themes on these popular talk shows, and ask yourself, what's *really* empowering about this. Telling a mother that her drug-addicted, out-of-control teen daughter just needs a makeover is *not* empowering.

Telling women who are extremely overweight, and who have obvious eating disorders that may lead to severe health issues in the future, that they are "fat and all that," is *not* empowering. Encouraging three- and four-hundred-pound women to perform striptease routines on a daytime talk show is not empowering.

Ladies: You can't be a four-hundred-pound stripper. You might start swinging around on a pole, and mess around and have a heart attack.

Other daytime shows let young girls think that it's OK to sleep with ten guys, and not know who their baby's daddy is. This is *not* empowering. Daytime commercials that tell women that the best way to predict their financial future is to contact the psychic hotline are *not* empowering. Telling women to have a spirit medium contact a dead relative so they can tell you if you are going to get married soon is *not* empowering.

See, there is profit in dysfunction. It's not in the best interest of these media outlets to tell women the truth.

Because the truth is empowering.

And if women really became empowered, these media out-lets wouldn't be able to sell women on all the BS that's splat-tered across television each day. These outlets promote dys-functional behavior, then turn around and provide their solutions to remedy the problems that they themselves help perpetuate.

So instead of telling women who are obese the truth—that overeating usually stems from emotional or psychological issues that they need to deal with—they tell women that they need to try the "forty-eight-hour miracle diet," or any other one of the quick-fix weight-loss remedies that contribute to the $50-billion-a-year diet product industry.

If you look very closely at those paternity shows on TV, you'll see they never promote birth control for women. You will always hear them say, "If the man wore a condom, he wouldn't be in this situation." But they *never* advise women to use birth control. They know that if a female is sleeping with five or six different guys, at least one of them isn't going to wear a condom. So she's putting *herself* at risk. It would be more logical to advise these women to use some form of birth control, so they won't put themselves in this type of situation. But these shows *want* women to be in these situations. Why? Because they need more guests for their shows. By using the blame-a-man tactic on these paternity shows, the women feel justified in their reckless sexual behavior. And they will con-tinue to engage in it, because there is no immediate negative backlash or criticism.

Some of these shows even run commercials for a child sup-port collection agency called Support Kids. So you see how these outlets always seem to have *solutions* to every paternity issue. At the end of these paternity shows, there's always a number for viewers to call if they are in need of a paternity test themselves. These paternity tests usually run between $500 and $600, so there is a lot of money in the "Who's my baby daddy?" business.

These media outlets want people to continue to have a bunch of kids irresponsibly, so they can have them on as guests, and so they can keep getting that DNA money.

Daytime television usually features three categories of men:

1. The doofus jackass

2. The hoodlum

3. Prince Charming

The doofus jackass is often the spineless, stone-faced guy who can't defend himself. Whenever he is getting clowned by his female counterpart, the talk-show host, or audience members, he drops his head and submits to his verbal lashing.

The hoodlum is the hip-hop cat with a cold, heartless disposition. He is the guy who is sneaking around and playing a number of different women. Whenever they do lie detector shows, the hoodlum fails all the test questions (which causes his female counterpart to break down crying and run offstage), and he is the main guy featured on the paternity shows.

The Prince Charming is a concoction of the media outlets. He is presented as *their* solution to the doofus jackass and the hoodlum. He is generally presented in the form of the sensitive male talk-show host, or he is the knight in shining armor on daytime soap operas.

The placement of the Prince Charming image is very effective in giving women unrealistic expectations about relationships. And there are some women who get so caught up with these soap operas, they don't even know how to draw the line between fantasy and reality. We've all known people who talk about soap opera characters as if they were real people. And once you have people so wrapped up that they can't differentiate between fiction and reality, you can literally sell them anything.

A few years ago, I read in *TV Guide* about a highly rated daytime soap called *Passions*. This show was very popular at the time, so I decided to check it out. So I'm watching this show, and it seems pretty normal. There was a couple lying in bed discussing their relationship. Typical soap opera stuff. Then all of a sudden, a midget named Timmy walked into the room. And the midget had *magical powers*. Timmy began to cast a spell on the couple. As I watched this, the only thing I could think to myself was, *"This is some of the stuff that women are watching?"* People will rarely admit to watching this nonsense, but it is still one of the highest rated daytime soaps, so *somebody's* watching it.

It is no wonder why so many women are frustrated with the lack of proper communication in their relationships. It is no wonder why so many women have unrealistic views about dating. You can't engage in proper communication or have realistic expectations about your relationships if you are sitting there watching Timmy the midget every day.

And women's magazines are another outlet that sell women these quick-fix solutions. The messages they send are "If you are depressed about a man, buy *this* outfit." "If you have low self-esteem, wear *this* make up." "If you are feeling empty inside, wear *this* hairstyle and try *these* hair products."

Even though many of these magazines throw in their token self-esteem articles, the *real* message they are sending is always at the forefront. Sure they might include a patronizing article, telling women it's OK to be big boned, and to "love the skin you're in." But on every other page, the nonverbal message is, "You ain't shit if you don't look like Tyra Banks or any other one of these models, and if you want to look like a super-model, and be the shit, buy *our* products."

Agencies with a Legal or Political Agenda and Misguided Feminism

Now the basic principles of modern feminism started off on point. In the late 1960s and early '70s, women's groups rallied for equal pay, equal education, and an end to discrimination. This is commonly referred to as *equity feminism*, and I personally (like most men) don't have a problem with equity feminism. As a matter of fact, I *encourage* it. Especially when it comes to dating. If you want to be an equal contributor to the relationship, go right ahead ladies. (Give me one of those feminist petitions, I'll sign it with you.) If you want to date me, and help out with some of these bills, be my guest. (Give me one of those picket signs, and I'll march right along with you.) If you want to get out of the house and work, I'll give you gas money.

The feminist movement took a wrong turn in the form of *gender feminism*. The gender feminists are the radical, extreme left, man-hating feminists who claim that women should not only be treated equally, but they should receive *preferential* treatment.

Gender feminists feel this way because their philosophy is that *all* women are victims of the evil male patriarchal society. (If you read any feminist propaganda, replace the term "patriarchy" with "evil men," and you will get a clear understanding of where they are coming from).

The heart of the gender feminist movement is the lesbian movement (by their own admission). This is at the root of the male bashing, blame-a-man philosophy. It was easy for them to use men as the scapegoat for everything negative that happens in women's lives.[1]

During the late '60s, the feminist groups were in the same category as a number of other organizations that were protesting the Vietnam War and rallying for prison reform, environmentalism, rights for Mexican Americans, civil rights for blacks, and the like. Because of their dissatisfaction with the status quo, many of these groups weren't too concerned with validity. They were here-today-gone-tomorrow type organizations.

But the radical feminists became vocal enough, and organized enough, to put politicians into office, and legislation into play, that would support and execute some of their feminist ideology. So a lot of these radical feminist views didn't become popular because they were hip and on point. A lot of feminist ideology came to the forefront because it was *enforced* by government legislation.

Once the gender feminists put politicians into office, and received government funding to create foundations to *help* women, they only needed one more thing: *victims*. If you are going to get government money to start an organization to help women, you have to have a lot of victims in order to justify receiving funding on a continuous basis. So the gender feminists helped create a victim mentality among women, with the promise of securing minute financial benefits.

The feminists began to tell women, "If someone at your job says to you, 'That's a nice outfit you are wearing,' that's not a compliment, that's *sexual harassment,* and we can get you some money." The feminists told women, "If you go out and get drunk, and have sex with eight different guys, you're not a stank ho, that's *date rape,* and we can get you money."

The feminists told women, "If you have four kids by four different guys, it's not *your* fault. They got you pregnant, and we can make them step up to the plate and get you money."

Not only do these "cry wolf" tactics not help women, they actually harm women as a whole, because they take attention away from women who *really* need help. If a woman is seriously experiencing pressure and anxiety at her job because she is *really* being sexually harassed, she might not be able to get the attention she needs because there are a bunch of other female opportunists making frivolous claims, trying to make a quick buck.

Encouraging women to cry wolf about sexual assault doesn't help women whatsoever. All it does is minimize the seriousness and viciousness of rape. A woman who has *really* been raped or violated is less likely to be taken seriously because a whole list of alcoholic hoes are pressing false charges, so they won't feel stank about themselves.

If a woman is going through a divorce, and she needs temporary financial assistance until she gets back on her feet, she can't get it, because there is a five-year waiting list for Section 8 and other government programs. And it takes so long to receive some of these government benefits because there are second- and third-generation hoodrats and chickenheads sitting around poppin' out kids, squandering these government resources.

And children are merely pawns in the eyes of gender feminists and government agencies. These agencies figured out that the easiest way to get support from the masses is to cater to a woman's basic, maternal instinct. They do this by claiming to do things for the benefit of children.

Many organizations use this tactic to solicit funds.

When certain charities want people to send in money, they will run commercials that feature starving children with flies all over them. During election time, when politicians are doing their smear campaigns against each other, they will run commercials claiming "My opponent voted to have toxic landfills put near schools. So don't vote for him, because he's trying to harm your children."

Gender feminists try to use these "benefit the children" tactics, but if you take a close look at their ideology, you will begin to realize that many gender feminists secretly *despise* children. Ladies, do you honestly think that these hard-core, lesbian feminists really like children? Having children represents everything these gender feminists are against.

One of their biggest complaints was that housework for women is oppressive, and that women should not be "barefoot, pregnant, and in the kitchen."

Gender feminists also asserted that women don't need a man, and that *all* heterosexual sex is a form of rape. This ideology was implied and popularized by feminist writers such as Andrea Dworkin and Catherine MacKinnon. They also complained that women shouldn't have to cook and clean, and so on. These complaints were the main rallying cries of the feminist movement. Well, to have children, you *have* to have sex with a man, and you *have* to be pregnant. When you have children, you *have* to cook and clean. So, to gender feminists, children represent oppression.

This is why they were so gung-ho about being pro-choice.

Abortion rights are a major feminist platform, and this is one of the many areas where the gender feminists contradicted themselves. They claimed to be pro-child and pro-choice. That's like saying "We love kids, and we want to help them, but if you don't want them, it's OK to kill them." Validation of this mentality was evident when one of the biggest (if not the biggest) of the feminist organizations, the National Organization for Women (NOW), strongly supported, and even helped set up a legal fund for Andrea Yates, the Texas mother who drowned her five children.

And these feminist groups, with the help of government legislation, have successfully made the father's role in a child's life obsolete. The government gives single mothers all types of financial incentives (free food, free medical, free housing), with one specific catch: They can't receive these benefits as long as a man is living in the household. Statistics show that children who are raised in fatherless homes are more likely to drop out of school, more likely to commit crimes, more likely to get pregnant at a young age, more likely to be incarcerated at an early age.[2] The list goes on and on.

If convincing women that they don't need a man and creating a generation of potentially dysfunctional children will help gender feminists reach their agenda, their attitude is "so be it."

And the government legislators make their money on the front end *and* the back end. They get financing to promote single parenthood. And when some of these potentially dysfunctional children grow up and become dysfunctional adults, these same government legislators will make more money by prosecuting and incarcerating them. So for these agencies, it's a win-win situation.

How Feminism Affected White Women and Black Women

When feminism first hit the mainstream, it was a vehicle for many middle-aged white women who needed attention to have their opinions heard. They began to recruit black women by telling them to look beyond race, and to become sisters in the struggle. These white women told black women things like "You don't need a man," and "You can be independent."

One of the differences between the white feminists and the black feminists was that white women knew better than to believe their own bullshit. At the same time, black women fell for this "I don't need a man" nonsense hook, line, and sinker.

Even Gloria Steinem, who helped create the "women don't need men" fallacy, didn't believe her own bullshit. Eventually, she contradicted all of her rhetoric and got married to a man herself.

Black women eventually did realize the "I'm independent" and "I don't need a man" philosophy was bullshit, but out of stubbornness, they stuck with it anyway, to save face.

If you notice, you hardly ever hear white women publicly announcing that "I'm independent" and "I don't need a man." But these are common catchphrases in the black female community (sistas even make songs about this). The irony of all this is that the same white women who convinced sistas to disregard the men in their lives, and be independent, turned around and gathered all them single black men up for themselves. Now, the sistas are complaining that white women are taking all the good black men.

So the reality is this. Women in general (black women in particular) have been tricked. Bamboozled. Run amuck. Led astray.

Now that we have uncovered the *real* root of the problem,

you can disregard all the Culture of Victimhood misinformation, and begin to tighten up your game.

Tip #6 on how women can have game:

Don't believe the hype. Be comfortable in knowing that you have the power to accumulate true knowledge and the game you need to improve yourself.

The less comfortable you are with yourself, the more insecure you will be around others. It's totally up to you to build your confidence.

7: Male/Female Promiscuity: The So-Called Double Standard

One thing I've noticed over the years is that whenever a female is confronted about sleeping with a number of different men, she usually has one answer (if she does actually admit to having multiple partners). She says, "If men can do it, why can't women?"

So why is there this double standard? Why is it that men who have multiple sex partners are considered studs, ladies' men, or players, and women who have multiple sex partners are considered sluts and hoes?

First of all, promiscuous sex affects men and women differently. For women, sexual promiscuity has emotional ramifications *and* physical ramifications. It's not in a woman's nature to have multiple sex partners. Women are *internal* creatures. The female sexual organ is on the *inside* of her body.

Men are *external* creatures. And the male sexual organ is on the *outside* of his body. Women are more sexually intrigued by things they hear or feel, or things that touch them emotionally, such as whispered sweet-nothings. Men are more sexually aroused by things they can physically see, such as a cute face, big breasts, or nice booty.

When a man engages in sex, many times it's just a physical form of recreation, and that's it. It's no different from playing football or throwing darts. It's just a way to achieve an orgasm.

Men mostly don't develop an emotional attachment through sexual intercourse. Men become emotionally attached to a woman based on other things she can bring to the table. Men also become emotionally attached to women based on things like her loyalty or dedication.

But for women it is inevitable that they'll become emotionally attached to someone who is literally going up in her body. When a man is having sex with a woman, he has physical molecules, DNA, and other bodily fluids intertwining with hers. So he literally leaves a part of himself inside that woman.

It's very difficult to detach yourself, emotionally, from a person who is physically going into your body (especially on a consistent basis). This is why women seem more emotional about relationships, especially ones that involve sex.

I believe that this is a biological issue, as well as a gender issue, because some gay *men,* who have other men going up in their bodies when they engage in sexual intercourse, act more emotional than some women.

Are You in a Relationship, or a Long-Term Booty Call?

Many women today have a "if a man can do it, women can do it too," mentality when it comes to everyday activities. This includes having casual sex. Some women are almost antagonistic in having this mentality. It's like many women are saying "We can do everything you guys can do, so there!"

The reality is this, ladies: many men are actually *cool* with this. As a matter of fact, many men wish women would back up these words more often. Most men think like this: "If you want to take me out to dinner for a change, please feel free to do so." And if you want to come over to the crib, just so you can get your freak on, with no strings attached, well come on over.

Many relationships start off as booty calls. The man and woman willingly consent to having sex with no attachments. No one tricked or manipulated anyone into doing anything they didn't want to do. Both parties agreed to just get their freak on every now and then. And many women are cool with this—at first.

Some women will try to go that extra mile to play the unemotional, unattached role, by going to the man's crib, having sex with him, and leaving directly afterwards. Now in her mind, the woman might be thinking, "I'm going to make him feel used like men make women feel after getting some booty." But in reality, ladies, what the men are really thinking is, "Thank goodness, she's leaving. Now I don't have to give her the courtesy cuddle. I can just roll over and go to sleep."

Like I said before, men put women in either the potential girlfriend category or the potential sex partner category. And a man can have a casual sex relationship with a woman for years. He can be content with that as long as she is. A man will keep a woman as a booty call as long as her emotional baggage or emotional input doesn't outweigh his desire to have sex with her.

But when a woman is having a casual sex relationship with a man over a period of time, it is inevitable that she will become emotionally attached to that man. This causes problems in that relationship. The female will think the man is feeling the same way she is beginning to feel about the relationship. And because she is becoming more emotionally involved, she expects *him* to want to make a deeper commitment to the relationship. But to the man, it's still just sex.

This leads to a lot of frustration in the relationship, because the man is getting his basic needs met, yet the woman is feeling unfulfilled. This brings us to:

Play or Be Played Rule #4

The way you start off in a relationship is the way you will end up in a relationship.

The men don't feel like they have done anything wrong, because having sex with no strings attached was something that *both* of them consented to. So when the women start coming at men like "I want more out of this relationship," the men are usually thinking, "Hey . . . I like the arrangement we already have."

The woman thinks they have established a "relationship," while the man still thinks that she is just a booty call. And trying to get a man to change the status of a booty call is like trying to get an NBA player to change his contract during the playoffs. The man is thinking "If I'm already winning, why renegotiate?"

How to Tell if a Man Is Just Interested in Sex with You

Ladies, when you go out on a date with a man, and you find that you don't like him, you will pretty much let it be known that you aren't feeling him. But when a man is out with a female, and he knows that the date isn't going to turn into a relationship, he will still smile in your face and act like he's interested.

A man can be out with a woman who is a complete nut case, but he will act like everything is cool, because he's thinking, "Maybe I can still hit that." Ladies, as you all well know, when a man is interested in you, he wants to have sex with you eventually. That's a given. But when he's *only* interested in sex from you, he will go out of his way to not rock the boat. He will sit there and agree with everything you say.

Play or Be Played Rule #5

If a man agrees with everything you say,
no matter how far-fetched or unusual it is,
he just wants to have sex with you.

It's one thing to put your best foot forward when you first meet someone. But when a guy starts to overdo it, that should be a red flag. If a man is interested in a relationship with you, he will be somewhat objective. He will voice his *real* opinions on certain issues, and he might even disagree with you here and there. But when he's being *too* cooperative with you, he's trying not to jeopardize his chances of getting the cooch.

When a guy is agreeing and going along with everything a woman says, the woman may mistake this as having good chemistry with the guy. Here's a quick way to test the situation whenever you are out with a new guy.

When you are having a conversation with your new guy, and he is agreeing with everything you say, express an opinion that you *know* is off the wall. Then watch his reaction. Say something like "I was reading something the other day that suggested that some U.S. presidents were really sent here from other planets. And you know what, I kind of agree with that. What do you think?"

Now if the guy you are on a date with is really interested in getting to know you beyond sex, he will look at you like, "What the hell are you talking about?" But if he's a guy who just wants to get some ass, he will agree with you, and probably say something like "I think that is true, because I have a cousin from Jupiter."

If a man agrees with whatever you say, even if it's nonsense, he's just trying to go along with the program long enough to get you to drop the drawers. So always pay attention to the nonverbal language.

What Constitutes Being a Ho?

I was driving on my way home one night, and a homeboy of mine called me on my cell phone, sounding real amused and excited about something. He said "Yo, King Flex, man, you gotta come over to the crib right now. There's something you've got to see." So I made a detour to his crib, just to quench my curiosity.

So I get over to his house, and I hear the music pumping as I walk in the front door. In the living room, there are about ten to fifteen guys, all sitting and lying around with their pants unzipped and down to their ankles, and there are condom wrappers scattered all across the floor. And these guys all look like they're worn out.

Then I see a very attractive young female, about twenty-two or twenty-three, sitting in the middle of the living room floor, naked, with a bed sheet half covering her body. She was just nonchalantly bobbing her head to the music with her eyes closed, as if she was "rolling" off of an Ecstasy pill or some other intoxicant.

Come to find out, this girl had just had sex with *every* guy in the room. Not only did she have sex with all the guys, she had sex with them two or three times over. That's why the guys were looking so worn out. And the female was still requesting more guys! This is why my homeboy was trying to call people over.

Now, you know me—I'm a hustler about my shit, first. I pulled this female to the side (because I was gonna pop some pimpin' at her). I say to the young lady, "I bet you made a lot of money here tonight, didn't you?" and this woman has the nerve to get *offended.* She was like "Money? . . . Oh no . . . Uh-uh . . . I'm not a *ho."* I'm thinking, "This woman just had sex with fifteen guys, back to back, and she doesn't think she's a ho?"

Surprisingly, many women have this warped philosophy when it comes to the issue of what constitutes a ho. Women look at the issue from a moral standpoint; and they make the mistake of thinking that morality comes into play when there is an exchange of money. But if you were to look at hoin' as an issue of morality, the exchange of *money* doesn't make it immoral, the sexual *act* makes it immoral.

If a person was just *giving* away free crack cocaine, and someone stepped to him and said "Hey, why don't you *sell* some of that cocaine?" the person who was giving away the crack couldn't turn around and say, "Oh no, I can't *sell* crack . . . That would make me a drug dealer. And that would be immoral."

There is a difference between a *ho* and a *prostitute*. A *ho* is a woman with multiple sex partners. A *prostitute* is a woman who has sex for money. There are a lot of hoes out there. And many hoes have the nerve to try and look down on prostitutes. I have more respect for a woman who is out there spittin' game for her paper than I do for a female who has slept with every rapper on BET and all she got out of the deal is a Roc-A-Wear T-shirt.

Now I know that many of you ladies are probably saying, "Well, what about men? Aren't there some men who are hoes too?" Absolutely. Sure there are men who are hoes. But the difference between a male ho and a female ho is that a man can sleep with three women in one week, and still be able to look *himself* in the mirror and *accept* his hoish-ness. When a woman does something like sleep with three men in one week, she will get into self-denial to try to justify why she's *not* a ho.

Women have "don't count" sex. After they engage in casual or promiscuous sex, they tell themselves things like:

"I was drunk, so that don't count."

"I'm visiting from out of town, so that don't count."

"I didn't *plan* on having sex when I went to his house, so that don't count."

"I think somebody put something in my drink at the club, so that don't count."

Many women have had promiscuous sexual experiences, but because of the shame they feel about it afterwards, they will try and block the experience out of their minds and pretend it didn't happen.

The Origin of Shame Associated with Female Promiscuity

Like I mentioned before, men having multiple sex partners may have moral ramifications, but women having multiple sex partners has moral, psychological, and biological ramifications. When women have multiple sex partners, the issue of paternity comes into play. This is why female promiscuity has been looked down upon since the beginning of time.

According to pimp folklore, Eve was tricked into having sex with the serpent, after which she gave birth to two children, Cain and Abel. Cain was believed to be the son of Satan, and because Cain came from an evil bloodline, he himself became the personification of evil. And since Cain was treated differently by his family and God, he became resentful of his more favored brother, Abel, and eventually killed him.

Similarly, a woman who has had multiple children with different men will react to the children differently, based on the relationship she has (or had) with each child's father. When one of the children misbehaves, mothers in this situations can sometimes say things like "You are just like your no-good daddy" or "You act just like your triflin' father."

The Paternity Issue

When a woman has multiple sex partners within a short period of time, the likelihood of her becoming pregnant becomes greater. Sperm cells can live in a woman's body for up to five days.[3] And when there are different groups of sperm cells, from a number of different men, in a woman's body, the sperm cells will actually work harder to compete with one another to reach the woman's egg. Now ladies, there is no way you can't feel stank about yourself, knowing that you have a relay race going on in your vagina.

Society has always looked down on promiscuous women, mainly because of the issue of paternity. Not knowing who their biological father is has emotional and medical ramifications for children.

If a child is born with a certain disease or medical condition, it is important to be able to trace the child's lineage to see if there's a genetic connection. Even today, if a child just happens to need a blood transfusion or an organ donated from one of his parents (or relatives on his father's side), and the man who is supposed to be his father is really not his father, the kid is ass-out.

A recent study from the American Blood Association revealed that DNA tests involving couples with children showed that 30 percent of the men in question were proven *not* to be the biological fathers. *Thirty percent*—that's a lot. This is why I say male/female promiscuity is a *so-called* double standard. Because now there is scientific proof that some women sleep around just as much as some men.

Is There Really a Double Standard?

In our society, we always hear things like, "Teenage boys are allowed to play the field and have sex, but teenage girls aren't allowed to do that." This is a load of BS. When teenage boys are out there having sex, they aren't doing it with each other. They are doing it with *teenage girls.*

The reality is that this double standard hasn't been enforced for years. As long as I can remember, there have always been laid-back guys and there have always been poon-hounds. And there have always been good girls and there have always been stank hoes.

One of the differences between a male ho and a female ho is that a man who is sleeping around will usually carry himself in a presentable manner. His playing the field doesn't have a visible effect on his outward appearance. But you can usually spot a female ho from a mile away.

In many cases, these females carry themselves like hoes. They might have a bunch of piercings, a dozen tattoos, or hoochie outfits. Whatever it is, their appearance reflects the way they feel about themselves. And many hoish women really don't feel good about themselves.

The only thing that stops many women from engaging in hoish behavior is the negative stigma behind it. But once these females are in an environment where the stigma is removed (like Mardi Gras, Cancun, or hoochie nightclubs), these women will act as hoish as possible.

There is no double standard any more. If you go to certain clubs today, you will see many bisexual females on the dance floor, doing things to each other that *men* wouldn't even do to women on the dance floor.

The reality is, our society promotes hoish behavior in young females. These days, society even has hoish role models. Take a real good look at some of the female entertainers and role models that many young girls look up to today (and there are hoish role models for almost every ethnic group).

Whenever an award show is on TV, these female "role models" try to out-stank each other. When J-Lo shows up at an award show wearing three pieces of cloth disguised as a dress, girls look up to that. When Toni Braxton shows up wearing a cut-off dress with her ass cheeks hanging from the side, girls look up to that. When Christina Aguilera shows up ass-naked, girls look up to that. When Lil' Kim shows up with one of her titties literally hanging out, girls look up to that. So I say, where is the double standard? Because the message to young girls these days is *if you act hoish, you might become rich and famous.*

Being hoish satisfies the primal need of getting attention for some women. And when women are starving for attention, any attention, whether good or bad, will suffice. Nowadays, girls are programmed to have a hoish mentality starting at a young age.

We have all seen situations where little three- and four-year-old girls are dancing while listening to music or watching a video, and the mothers are telling the girls things like "Go 'head and shake your booty baby," or "Drop it like it's hot for mama, boo-boo." So the message these girls learn at a very young age is that hoochie behavior will get them positive affirmations.

These girls carry this mentality into middle school and then high school. We have all seen how raunchy and stank some middle school and high school cheerleading teams from inner city schools can get.

I saw something on the news recently about a committee in North Carolina that was planning their annual Thanksgiving Day parade. Now, in these parades they have high school cheerleading teams participating. On this occasion the committee actually had to approach one school's administration to tell them that their cheerleaders were so raunchy they would have to tone it down a bit for the next parade.

The committee was mainly concerned about the small children who were in attendance. The year before, these cheerleaders had come out half-dressed in hoochie outfits, and they turned the parade into a strip show. And it's kind of disturbing to be sitting with your family, watching a parade go by, and you see a pilgrim . . . a turkey . . . a tittie.

Ironically, the cheerleaders' *mothers* were actually upset that their daughters were told to tone themselves down. These mothers were actually fighting for their daughters' right to be hoish, and this isn't just an isolated incident. This type of behavior in young girls is promoted across the board (mainly by their own mothers). When these girls grow up and want to get jobs at strip clubs, then these parents will whine "Where did I go wrong?"

How Hoin' Affects Society

One of the problems with our society's current acceptance of hoishness is that many decent women sometimes get lumped in the same category with the hoochies. You can go to the club, and there could be two hundred classy and respectable women there, but if two stank hoes show up, it will change the whole tone of the club.

Ladies, you have all been to a place where some raunchy

women started showing out, and all of a sudden, the guys in the place started looking at you like you might be raunchy too. This is why most top-notch women can't stand stank hoes. Classy women have more contempt for these women than men do.

A friend of mine, a photographer, was hired to videotape a party thrown by an NBA player in his Beverly Hills mansion. We were looking at the footage, and the party seemed very laid back and mellow at first. There were a lot of conservative and decent-looking women in attendance. Then the camera zoomed in on these three stanks who came in the party.

These hoochies started to give guys lap dances, and one of the women was even caught on tape performing oral sex on a guy—in front of everybody at the party! The camera panned back across the room, and all the top-notch women had looks of shock on their faces. Some of these women were actually running for the door trying to get out of there.

As I'm watching the tape, I recognize one of the women at the party. This woman is a very straightlaced, nine-to-five, marketing director at a major entertainment company. I happened to run into her a few weeks later, and I mentioned I had seen a tape of the party she'd been at in Beverly Hills. She grabbed me and said, "Tariq, *please* don't tell nobody I was at that party!! Did you see them nasty hoes?"

This attitude is indicative of many non-hoochie women in our society. Most decent women don't want to be remotely associated with stank hoes. This is why most hoish women have to stick with and confide in other hoish women (this is also one of the reasons we have the current bisexuality trend among females).

Again, hoish behavior all boils down to getting male attention. And this brings us to:

Play or Be Played Rule #6

All men love hoes—just not as girlfriends or wives.

Many women say that this too is a double standard, because a woman can forgive a man who is sleeping around on her, but if a woman is sleeping around on a man, he doesn't want anything to do with her. This is true simply because the consequences are different for the men and women involved.

Now I don't try to justify deceptive behavior in men whatsoever. I'm totally against a man being dishonest and sleeping around on his wife or girlfriend. I don't think a man should even make a serious commitment to a woman if he's really not ready to settle down. But if a man is in a serious or committed relationship, and he is still out there hoin' around, for the most part, his hoish behavior will only affect *him* (unless he's out there contracting some kind of disease). Some women might suffer some emotional pain behind his hoish behavior but, for the most part, their physical and general well-being will still be intact.

But if a man is in a relationship with a hoish woman, this could have a direct impact on everything in his life. And this goes back to the paternity issue. It is the law in this country, based on a five-hundred-year-old common law agreement originating in Europe, that any child a woman gives birth to while she is married automatically becomes the legal responsibility of the husband. This is called presumption of paternity. So if a married woman gets pregnant as the result of an affair, and the husband has DNA proof that the child is not his, he still has a legal obligation to that child.

Today, the courts are flooded with cases of men having to give money to women for children that aren't even theirs. In

California, if a woman simply puts down a man's name as the father of a child, it's up to the man to prove that he's not the father. If he doesn't do so in a certain amount of time, he will lose the paternity case by default. And there are guys who have liens put on their homes, their wages garnisheed, and their lives turned upside down, paying for a female's hoish behavior.

So a man has a lot more to lose when dealing with a female who is hoish. But women don't get off scot-free with their hoish behavior either. Many women don't want the stigma or title of being a ho, but they want the *benefits* of hoin'. And no matter how much you deceive yourself, you can't have one without the other.

Even though there are instant incentives that come with promiscuous behavior in women (attention, money, gifts), the long-term effects are damaging. Like we say in the game, *hoes have a shelf life.* Society uses hoes for two things: sexual gratification and money. And once a ho isn't sexually desirable anymore, or she isn't able to be used for profit anymore, she is discarded.

So ladies, if you want to use the myth of the so-called double standard between men and women to justify having multiple sex partners, society may give you the green light to do so (society might even give you incentives to do so). However, ultimately, *you* will suffer from the long-term consequences.

Which brings us to a very important issue regarding promiscuous behavior . . .

The Pregnancy Hustle

What I'm about to discuss here will probably rattle a few nerves. Some of it may even offend the faint of heart. But this is an issue that must be talked about in an honest manner for once. And for the first time in modern literature, the issue of the pregnancy hustle will be addressed in a realistic manner.

In our society, we have *way* too many single mothers in general, and way too many teen mothers in particular. The United States has the largest number of teen pregnancies in the world.[4] And the reason this epidemic has gone on for so long, and reached the proportions it has reached, is because society isn't addressing the *real* root of the problem.

For the last thirty years, society has been focusing on one side of the problem: the fathers who aren't involved in their children's lives. Now, I believe that if a man has a child, he should take responsibility for that child. However, a man should not assume that the female he is having sex with is taking birth control. Even if the woman says she is, the man should still be cautious. Because too many men are too quick to trust the females they meet.

Whatever actions men choose to take in life, they must also deal with the consequences of those actions. And if they do have children, they should take care of their seeds.

The problem with the single-parent phenomenon today is that society has been placing all the focus on the deadbeat-dad stereotype. For years, we have been hearing how these no-good men go around and victimize women by "getting" them pregnant, and then abandon the women and their responsibilities.

And when the topic of single parenthood comes up, we always hear the same empty clichés such as "Men need to step up to the plate," and "Anybody can make a baby, but it takes a real man to be a father," and on and on. All this is rhetoric and bullshit. And deep down, most women *know* this is bullshit, and it's time to stop dancing around the single-parent issue.

Contrary to the feminists, contrary to the government, contrary to popular belief, the idea that you don't need no man to raise a baby is just not cutting it. Because based on results, the single parent phenomenon isn't working. Statistics from all across the board have shown the negative outcome of having fatherless children. The jails and crackhouses are filled with fatherless men, and the ho-strolls and strip clubs are filled with fatherless women. The list of how fatherlessness affects people growing up can go on and on. We all know the results.

Too many women are led to believe that the "I can raise a child by myself" mentality is somehow empowering to women. The notion of getting pregnant and raising children without a father has become almost a badge of honor among many women in our society. Well, I have news for you ladies—it's not.

This is one of the biggest con games that society plays on women. And now we have women who con themselves with this mentality. Because raising a child and raising a child *properly* are two different things. Purposely putting children in a situation that is most likely to be dysfunctional isn't beneficial to the children, and it isn't beneficial to society.

The Real Reason Behind the Single Mother Phenomenon

It's funny to hear the "experts" trying to figure out the cause of the teen-mother/single-parent epidemic. There are many sex education programs available. There are different forms of birth control available (at least ten different forms of birth control for women). They even have the new RU-486 morning-after pill for women. There are so many alternatives to becoming a parent, yet more and more women are getting pregnant at a younger age.

The reason none of these programs or these other alternatives have been working is because contrary to popular belief, most women don't get pregnant by accident. Most women get pregnant because they *want* to get pregnant. Let's keep it real, ladies. No one can "get" you pregnant. You *allow* yourself to get pregnant. Because women who don't want to get pregnant, normally *don't get pregnant.*

There is a certain profile for women who just "happen" to get pregnant a number of times. It's usually F-class females (and some B-class females). The majority of females you see having a number of children at a young age are unattractive women with no game. If you want proof of this, go to any trailer park or housing project in the country, and you will see generation after generation of teenage females with a number of kids. When you see the baby-mama shows on daytime TV, who do you see? Chickenheads and trailer trash.

F-Class females get pregnant at a young age because they know early on that they will never achieve the education it takes to become a success on their own. And they know they don't have the looks to become a gold digger, and have Captain Save-A-Ho or Prince Charming come and save them. So to these women, getting pregnant and having a baby is like a consolation prize.

B-class females usually wait a little longer before they cash out and claim their consolation prize. Most F-class females cash out early (in their mid to late teens), but B-class females normally cash out in their mid to late twenties. B-class women try to use their looks to come up in life. And when those looks start fading, they hurry up and get pregnant, so at least they can use the child to hustle income for themselves. Some B-class women wait too long to have children, and when their biological clocks run out they are forced to deal with their own failures and mistakes they've made in life. Because now, they can't blame the guy who "got" them pregnant. A lot of females who have no game, and who don't cash out by having children in time, end up becoming bag ladies and crazy women.

How the Pregnancy Hustle Works

The pregnancy hustle is a game. It is a very strategic and calculating game that is played out by women who don't have any other form of game. As I said earlier, it is played out mainly by F-class females.

We all know the damaging long-term effects of teen pregnancies and single motherhood.[6] And we assume that the statistics of what happens with teen mothers would deter most young women from becoming one of these statistics.

The reason so many females are becoming teen mothers is that society gives these females *incentives* to become teen mothers. Like I said before, most people will settle for instant gratification and deal with the negative, long-term consequences later. Society tells F-class females—females who can't see a prosperous future or anything else going on in their lives—that if they just go out and get pregnant, they can get free housing, free food, free medical expenses, *and* they get to blame whoever the man was who "got them pregnant." These females feel like they hit the jackpot.

Now when it's time to deal with the reasons why women make the choice to become single mothers, many people are quick to deflect the blame back onto the men. We always hear things like "It takes two to tango," and "What about the man—he should be held responsible as well."

If you plan on robbing a bank, and you convince some guy

to be the getaway driver, and you happen to get caught robbing the bank, you can't say, "My getaway driver helped me do it, so punish him instead of me." Both of you are guilty. And if you were the mastermind of the robbery, you can't point the finger.

But in today's society, when it comes to the pregnancy hustle, the judicial system *does* punish the "getaway driver" and lets the "mastermind" off scot-free. This is why the pregnancy hustle is the perfect crime.

When a man has a child, he can be forced to take financial responsibility (women can give their children up for adoption, and not be held financially responsible). Also, if a man is told that he is the father of a child, and later finds out he's not, if he has signed any type of paternity documents, he still has to take financial responsibility, even for children that are not his. So men don't have to step up to the plate, because the plate will be brought straight to *them*.

In order to alleviate the pregnancy hustle, we have to address the masterminds of the hustle. Ladies, parenting (not getting pregnant) is a choice—not an accident, not a slip up, not a violation, but a choice over which you have 100 percent control.

Spouting clichés like "A man made the choice to become a parent the minute he had sex without a condom" is a cop-out. Men have no choices when it comes to reproductive rights. Men only have *risks*. And there's a difference between a *risk* and a *choice*. When a man has sex, he *risks* the possibility of getting a child (just as a person crossing the street has a *risk* of getting hit by a bus. This doesn't mean he chooses to get hit by a bus). Because even if a man *wants* to become a parent, and he's having sex with three or four women, *trying* to get them pregnant so he can have a child, he still doesn't have the choice of becoming a parent. That choice is ultimately up to the woman.

Other cop-out statements people use when discussing the pregnancy hustle issue are "If a man just stayed around and took care of his responsibilities, there wouldn't be so many single-parent homes," and "men shouldn't 'abandon' their 'families' after the women get pregnant."

These cop-out statements help many young women feed into the fallacy that having a baby will somehow keep a man. And I don't have to tell you how untrue that is.

The Pimp/Ho Aspect of the Pregnancy Hustle

There is a reason why the pregnancy hustle is legal and thriving in this country. It wouldn't be going on this long if someone wasn't benefiting from it. All of the participants *claim* that what they do is for the benefit of the children. The government implemented the current child support system in 1975, and cases of single-parent upbringing have been on the rise ever since.[7] I have yet to see any number of children who have benefited from the current child support system. (Children don't grow up and say "I grew up without a father, but it's OK, because the state got a percentage of my dad's check, so I'm fine now.") And I have already pointed out all the other consequences of what happens to many children from single-parent homes.

Since we see that the children are not benefiting from the pregnancy hustle, who does? Well, of course, F-class females. The government also gets its piece of the pie. The child support industry is a multi-*billion*-dollar industry.[8] There are judges, lawyers, mediators, child support enforcement agencies, and private collection agencies, who all work hand in hand with one another to keep the pregnancy hustle flowing.

If women were to actually stop becoming single parents, all these people would lose billions of dollars, and they are not about to let that happen. Therefore, they need as many dead-beat dads as they can get. Because the government gets a lot of money from garnisheeing these guys' wages. So the government encourages promiscuous behavior in women.

The government is like a pimp. And the government treats young women in this country as hoes, encouraging women to turn as many "tricks" as possible. The feminists are like the "madams," because a madam's job is to help a female justify her hoish behavior.

Plus the madam is the pimp's main lady, and she teaches the up-and-coming ho the ropes. Men in this country are looked upon as being the "johns" or "tricks," and children are merely used as bargaining chips. So the "hoes" are encouraged to appear as if they are offering the "johns" free, uncommitted sex. And after the sex act is over, the pimp comes in and forces the "john" or "trick" to pay for the sexual encounter.

And that's all child support is: payment for sex. Children are the last to benefit from "child support," if they do at all. The government wants women to sleep with as many people and get as many "baby daddies" as possible, so they can kick the females down with a few dollars and also get their cut.

This is why the government has made it perfectly legal for a woman to lie about the paternity of her child. If a man pays thousands of dollars in so-called child support, and later proves that he is not the actual father of the child, the woman cannot be prosecuted and the man cannot get his money back from the female or the government. If that's not a gangster pimp move by the government, I don't know what is.

The pregnancy hustle is a legal scam that our government allows young ladies to play on society and ultimately on themselves. And ladies, just because you can get away with something legally doesn't mean you should do it. Just because something is legal doesn't make it morally correct. Forty years ago, it was "legal" to prohibit black folks from drinking out of certain water fountains.

Fortunately, there were white folks who rose above that "privilege" and joined with blacks to abolish those type of laws. Thank goodness we have enough sistas out here in society today who have enough sense not to reduce themselves to laying up with a bunch of different people in order to get knocked up, so they can swindle a few dollars, simply because the opportunity is available.

Single Mothers and the Single Mother Mentality

For the record, let me say that I'm not knocking single mothers. I'm criticizing the single-mother mentality. And there is a difference. If you are a female who was in a committed marriage or relationship and you had children from that relationship, then later on down the line, you and your partner split up, for whatever reason, and you are raising your children the best you can, I have much love for you. That's a situation where you had no control over the outcome.

But if you are trying to get pregnant by going out and sleeping with every other guy you meet at the club, under the pretense of uncommitted sex, then a year later you're on the *Ricki Lake Show* with a stage full of guys, talking about "one of y'all need to step up to the plate," you gets no love.

Because you are not a victim, you are a volunteer.

Should all the parties involved be held accountable? Sure. The men are guilty of being naïve, and the women involved are guilty of being deceptive. And if a female has to trick somebody into procreating with her, she must be in really bad shape.

We've all seen the paternity shows on daytime TV, where there is a stage full of guys, crossing their fingers, hoping they are not the baby's daddy. And the female is sitting onstage with her mother, and the mother is portraying her daughter as a victim. This is part of the single-mother mentality.

If a female has a baby at seventeen, and her mother is thirty-two, and her grandmother is forty-eight, that's a single-mother mentality that has been passed down from generation to generation. And if you are a female who is in that cycle, you need to break that cycle. Sure, you can get temporary benefits and gratification (financial gain, attention, preferential treatment, and waived responsibility) from playing the pregnancy hustle, but the long-term consequences are going to hit you like a brick.

Because after you reach a certain age, no one wants to hear you play the victim role anymore. And if you continue to have this mentality, your dating options will be severely limited.

A woman who just happens to be a single mother, due to consequences beyond her control, will normally have no problem when it comes to getting into a significant relationship in the future. (Shaqille O'Neal's wife Shaunie had a son before she met Shaq. And his teammate Rick Fox married actress Vanessa Williams, and she had a *gang* of kids when she met Rick. So these two single mothers ended up with two of the richest athletes in the country.) But when a woman is trying to date, and she has that irresponsible, blame-a-man, "I'm a victim," single-mother mentality, any man of substance isn't going to give her the time of day.

And she will have to settle for dating parolees for the rest of her life. Because the single-mother mentality equates to *baggage,* and baggage is never an incentive for a man to date a woman.

So now you know the different consequences of male and female promiscuity. Ladies, you should never put yourself out there sexually because you want to be equal with men. Allowing a number of people to have sex with you is not an accomplishment. It doesn't make you equal. It makes you stank.

Because *any* woman can get somebody to have sex with her. There are two things that a woman is guaranteed to get in life: that's her *period* and a *penis.* Ladies, it's simple: if you give off ho vibes, you will receive ho reactions. And if you give off queen vibes, men will step to you like the queen you are.

Tip #7 on how women can have game:

Respect the laws of physics.

The first law of physics is that for every action, there is an equal or greater reaction. That means if you carry yourself with respect, people will treat you with respect. And if you act stank, people will treat you stank. Never try to use bullshit logic like "just because I dress half naked, that doesn't mean I should be disrespected." That goes against the laws of physics. If you don't respect yourself, don't complain when other people don't respect you either. You can't walk around with your ass out and expect men to treat you like you are Claire Huxtable.

8: The Real Reasons Why Some Men Cheat

We've all heard the same clichéd explanations on why some men cheat. "It's in a man's nature to cheat," "All men are dogs," "All men let their little head control their big head." Adopting these empty, blanket statements will only disable women from properly selecting a suitable mate.

We are going to look at the *real* reasons why men cheat. We will also look at the reasons why women choose to stay in relationships with cheaters.

First of all, there is no *one* reason why men cheat. If you ask twenty different guys why they cheat, you'll get twenty different reasons. Every man (just like every woman) has the *potential* to cheat, but generally we can break it down to eight *types* of cheaters. And these guys are the most common perpetrators of infidelity in committed relationships.

Types of Cheaters

The Rebellious Child Cheater

This cheater is the guy who is constantly getting into a mother-child relationship with women. This brotha feels powerless, because his woman is the dominant one in the relationship. He has a lot of internal conflicts, because he wants to be looked at as a man, but he's afraid to leave the comfort zone of a mother figure.

He's afraid of the responsibilities of manhood, so he regresses into the role of a child. He will often engage in childlike activities like excessive video game playing or bragging about the new sneakers he is going to get.

So a woman might be dating a guy who is twenty-eight years old, but he has the thought processes and reasoning of a fifteen-year-old. And this frustrates a lot of women. When someone has the biological appearance of an adult, it's only natural for you to deal with them on an adult level. But in the mind of a guy like this, he is still a child. And just like you don't expect mature, responsible behavior from a fifteen-year-old, you shouldn't expect any mature, responsible rational behavior from a grown man with a childlike demeanor.

Whenever this brotha is challenged or his powerlessness is acknowledged in some way by his woman, instead of trying to communicate and express himself like a rational adult, he does what many children do in these situations: He rebels.

This guy takes on the "I can do what I want to do" mentality, and he sneaks off and has sexual relations with other women. He does this strictly as an act of defiance. It is his way of indirectly showing his main woman that he cannot be controlled 100 percent.

The Delayed Player Cheater

When you don't complete something, you will want to finish it at some point in your life. And most men in our society have to go through their player stage. Some men get their player stage over with early in life, some guys go through it much later.

The delayed player (like the married mack described in chapter 3) is the guy who didn't get to go through his player stage during his teens and twenties, because he got married at a young age.

When he was young, he was so happy that a female gave him some play, he went on and tied the knot with her right away. Now that he's older, more established, and more financially stable, he is getting the kind of play from other women that he didn't get when he was younger.

So *now* he wants to go through his player stage, and get a taste of some of the other females that are out there on the market. But he still sincerely loves his wife and he doesn't want to leave her. This is also referred to as a midlife crisis.

These middle-aged guys will start purchasing fancy cars that they wished they had as a teenager. They start dressing in fly clothes they couldn't afford as a teen. And they start trying to have sexual relations with different females, which is also something they wish they could have done when they were teenagers.

The Playing-with-Fire Cheater

This type of brotha is motivated by the possibility of getting caught cheating. He is sexually turned on by the thrill and the danger of his acts of infidelity. This guy will cheat with his woman's sister or his wife's best friend.

He will have sex with other females in the same bed he and his wife or girlfriend sleep in. He will have sex with other women in his woman's car. The playing-with-fire cheater is usually a laid-back type of guy, who is extremely turned on by the fact that he is doing something naughty or devious.

He wishes he could be more adventurous in other aspects of his life, but he's not. So the only way he feels that he can get his thrills in life is to sneak around with other women, and toy with the possibility of getting found out.

The Free Agent Cheater

In sports, a free agent is an athlete who isn't under a specific contract, who can go to any team that chooses him. He can also go from playing baseball to playing football or any other sport he chooses. The free agent cheater is a guy who is in a marriage or committed relationship, but in his *mind* he is still a free agent. The marriage contract means absolutely nothing to him. It's just a piece of paper he signed to shut his main lady up.

The free agent cheater parades his other relationships out in the open as if he were still single. And he has absolutely no remorse in doing this, because in his mind he isn't doing anything wrong.

The Cheaper-to-Keep-Her Cheater

This type of guy is in a relationship or marriage that he knows has run out of gas. The relationship lost its sparks a long time ago, and he genuinely wants to end it so he and his significant other can go their separate ways. But he also knows that if he's the one who breaks the relationship off, his woman and her lawyers will take him to the cleaners.

He knows that officially ending his relationship and getting back in the dating scene means that he must lose his house, half his wages, and possibly his automobile. Starting a new life

means he would probably have to dramatically downgrade his standard of living. And he knows getting some new poon-tang isn't worth living in the projects for.

So he keeps the wife around under the pretense of having a "business arrangement." And he gets back into the dating scene with no remorse, because to him, his marriage is technically over anyway.

The Coochie Conquering Cheater

The only reason this type of guy gets into committed relationships is because he thinks it's the only way he can get a woman to have sex with him. He is intrigued by the thrill of the hunting process and of getting a sexual commitment from a woman. Once a woman finally gives in, he is no longer interested. He has conquered her coochie, and he is ready to move on.

But this guy has made so many commitments, and gone to such extravagant lengths in order to get the coochie, that now that he has finally gotten his payoff, he finds that he can't just jet out so quickly.

The coochie conqueror is a master deceiver and he will sell a dream to a woman with a straight face—all for the poon-tang. Then he will go on to other conquests, and still date his main woman, until he comes up with another lie or scheme to wiggle his way out of the relationship.

The Deflecting Guilt Cheater

This type of guy is in a relationship or marriage that he feels isn't bad enough to break off, but it isn't good enough to stay in either. And if he were to break the relationship off, he would feel a tremendous sense of guilt. So he becomes blatant with his cheating, in hopes that his main lady will find out, and decide to break up with him.

Another type of guilt deflecting cheater is a guy who has a decent woman at home, but he wants to get some extra poon on the side anyway. He feels guilty about his desires, so he will find any little thing about his woman that he can nitpick or complain about. He does this because he is looking for justification to go out and cheat. And if he can find some little thing that his woman has done "wrong," he doesn't feel as guilty when he goes out and commits his own wrongs.

The Take-Out Order Cheater

This guy is in a relationship where the woman uses sex as a bargaining chip. When the wife or girlfriend tries to deprive him of sex in order to manipulate him, he simply goes out and gets sex elsewhere.

He doesn't cheat to make a statement or to prove any kind of point. He cheats because he still needs his sexual needs met. These guys think like this: if there is no food in the house, a man isn't going to sit in the house and starve. He's going to go out and pick up something at a drive through, fast-food place.

And he has the same mentality when it comes to sex. If the sex supply has shut down at home, his sexual desires don't go away. So he goes out and gets "take-out order" sex from strippers, hookers, or call girls. A strip club is like a take-out food drive-through window to him: he just pulls up and places his order. "I'd like two titties and some ass please . . . and make that *to go*. Thank you." He does his deed, he goes back home, and it's back to the normal program.

Now that I have given an in-depth view of the common cheating-type men that are out there, we need to get into part two of this issue. Because there are women who will still date

these guys, knowing full well what they are capable of. So we are going to get into the issue of why many *women* enable these types of relationships.

How Women End Up in Relationships with Cheating-Type Men

One difference between a tornado and a hurricane is that a tornado is unpredictable, but a hurricane can be foreseen days in advance. And experts can usually predict the exact moment when a hurricane will strike.

A man's relationship with a cheating woman is like being in a tornado. A man wouldn't even *think* about having a committed relationship with a woman he thought was a potential cheater. He might assume that he's in a relationship with a good girl, but by the time he finds out that she wasn't what he thought she was, it's too late. All the damage has been done.

And he is taken completely by surprise, because men usually don't have a clue about how a cheating woman behaves.

But a woman dating a cheating man is like being in a hurricane. Women will meet a man and know that he has the potential to be a cheater, but they will date him anyway.

We've all seen news footage of places where a hurricane is about to strike, and everyone in the place is evacuating. But there is always *one* stubborn old person who lives in a house *right by the ocean,* who refuses to leave, in spite of the danger. You always see that one stubborn person on TV talking about how "I've been living here in my house for over thirty years, and I'm not going to let no Hurricane Andrew run *me* away."

You notice too that after the hurricane, you never see those stubborn people again. That's because the hurricane has blown their asses off into the Bermuda Triangle somewhere. And many women can foresee the potential danger of a cheating-type man when they first meet him, but out of stubbornness and defiance, these women will still pursue the relationship.

And again, I don't buy the "He wasn't like that when I met him" excuse. Women are fully aware of the potential danger of a cheating-type man when they meet him. As a matter of fact, that dangerous element is what intrigues women about these men in the first place.

Many women like men who are sort of rough around the edges. It's very gratifying to a woman's ego to know that she can tame a wild stallion, so to speak. Many Harlequin novels feature a sensitive woman who tames a lustful bad boy, and this is why these books are huge sellers among women. Many movies have the same theme as well; just check out *Deliver Us from Eva,* where LL Cool J plays a ladies' man and a major player who meets a strong-willed woman named Eva. By the end of the movie, Eva turns LL's character from a player to a sensitive, responsible, one-woman guy.

Ladies, this works in movies, and it works in Harlequin novels, but it rarely works in real life. Because the reality is, cheating-type men are like hurricanes. And it doesn't matter how much of a strong woman you think you are, no matter how much you pump yourself up by listening to empowering songs like "I Will Survive" and "I'm Every Woman." No matter how much you think you can stand up to the challenge of any man, you cannot conquer a hurricane. It will wipe you out every time.

And the thing about hurricanes, they oftentimes strike with *two* devastating impacts. Hurricanes are violent circular winds that form in the ocean, with a calm center—the eye. When a hurricane arrives on land, it wreaks destruction, and then there is a temporary calm as the eye of the storm passes over. Then the second strike comes and destroys what is left of the city.

The problem many women have with cheating-type men is that these women usually try to get help once they are in the *eye* of the storm. Because when a woman finds out her man is cheating, it has a devastating impact. She and her man may discuss his cheating, and when he promises he won't do it no more, she lets it slide, and things seem to go back to normal.

Everything will seem cool temporarily, but in the back of her mind, she knows that the second impact of the hurricane is coming at any moment. And when it does come, she knows that the second strike will fully destroy the relationship.

And many women wait until they get smack dab in the middle of a hurricane, and ask "How do I protect myself from being hurt by a cheater?" Well, the best form of security is prevention, because once you realize you are in the middle of a hurricane or a relationship with a cheating-type man, the best thing you can do is charge it to the game, start over, and rebuild. Then, learn what signs to look for when it comes to the next relationship.

Let's face it, ladies. When you first met that cheating-type man you had a relationship with (and many of you have been in relationships with such men), you *knew* he had six felonies . . . You *knew* he didn't have a good relationship with his other five baby mamas . . . You *knew* he was one strike away from being sent to prison for life . . . You *knew* he liked going to the strip clubs every weekend . . . You *knew* all this but you chose to date him anyway. All you did was train a bear. So don't act surprised when the bear attacks.

Many women are afraid of the first impact of being in a relationship with a cheating-type man, but they are even more terrified of the second impact, because the second impact means starting over and rebuilding. And most people hate having to walk away from an investment.

After you have put your time, focus, energy, and money into something, you hate to see it just go to waste without receiving some type of payoff. But if you have invested in a house, and then you find out that the house is built on quicksand, no matter how much money you continue to pour into the house, it's still going to sink. The best thing you can do is count your losses, and do a little more research before you reinvest.

Here's a few signs to look for to see if you might be in a relationship with a cheater. Some of these are obvious. Some of them are a little more subtle. Nevertheless, if you see any of these signs, you should consider them potential red flags.

Top ten signs you might be in a relationship with a cheater:

1. All of a sudden he starts working late.

2. He guards his cell phone like the secret service (so you won't pick it up if it rings, or so you don't look at the stored numbers).

3. He suddenly starts wearing new cologne and putting relaxers in his hair.

4. He starts "getting his workout on" at the gym all of a sudden.

5. He wants to try new freaky sexual acts on you out of the blue. (If he suddenly wants you to tie him up and pee on him, that's a real red flag.)

6. He seems to purposely start arguments or he nitpicks over petty things.

7. He suddenly starts hanging with known players and poon hounds.

8. He comes in the house acting extra nice all of a sudden.

9. He starts showering a lot.

10. If he says things like "I'm running to the grocery store real quick," but he has on "gators" and he's bling blingin', that's a red flag.

Why Many Women Stay with Cheaters

Oftentimes, when a woman is with a cheating-type man, she automatically internalizes his infidelity, as if she could or should have done something about it. In many cases, when a woman finds out that her man is cheating, she starts asking herself "Where did *I* go wrong," and "Why wasn't I good enough for him?"

This brings us to:

Play or Be Played Rule #7

When a man cheats, 80 percent of the time it has nothing to do with *you*.

That is just a part of who *he* is at the moment. And you cannot change or control a man's actions. You can only change and control your *reactions* to whatever a man brings to the table.

Thinking you can do something to stop a man from cheating is like thinking you can do something to stop it from raining outside. You can hope and wish that the rain will go away, but when it's raining outside and you have no umbrella, you have two choices: go inside where it's dry, or stay outside and get wet. And if you happen to encounter a cheating-type man, you have two choices: you can accept the infidelities and hope he stops lying, or you can move on to a better situation.

Never frustrate yourself by trying to rationalize a man's cheating using "if I" scenarios. ("He probably wouldn't have cheated 'if I' was taller, 'if I' was slimmer, 'if I' was prettier, 'if I' had a lot of money, 'if I' had firmer breasts," and so on.) You can be one of the finest and richest women in the world, and that still won't help you change a cheating-type man. Look at Halle Berry. Halle is one of the baddest women in the world, and her husband Eric Benet cheated on her.

Women stay in relationships with verified cheaters for a number of different reasons. They will come up with self-delusional excuses as to why they remain in these relationships. Here are the top three self-delusional excuses women give for staying in relationships with cheaters:

1. *The Investment Excuse:*
   "We've invested so much together."

2. *The Doing the Kids a Favor Excuse:*
   "We have kids together."

3. *The Spiritual Cop-out Excuse:*
   "The Bible said people shouldn't get divorced," or
   "He who is without sin shall cast the first stone."

Women have been using these excuses for years in order to justify staying in cheating relationships. But now, we are going to look at some of the *real* reasons why so many women stay in these relationships.

The Top Five Reasons Why Many Women *Really* Stay in Relationships with Cheaters

1. They are afraid to get out of the comfort zone.

Women become relaxed in relationships. When some women have been with a guy for a certain period of time, they feel like they don't have to put in as much maintenance as they did when they first met him. And a woman likes reaching the point in the relationship where she can let her guard down, and be herself around her man.

A woman has reached that point of comfort in the relationship when she can let her man see her without her weave, when she can fart in front of her man, when she can get naked without turning the lights off, or when she can act ghetto in front of her friends when her man is around.

So if she finds out her man is cheating, and she acknowledges the fact that she has to move on, this means she would have to get out of that comfort zone and start over again. And when you are trying to get into a new relationship, you now have to go through the trouble of putting your best foot forward. You have to keep your hair done. You have to go to the gym. You have to act sophisticated. You have to hold in those farts.

So in many cases, to avoid all the maintenance it takes to snag a new man, women will just find self-delusional reasons to justify staying in the comfort zone with the cheating man. (Remember what I said earlier about the instant gratification of being in a comfort zone.)

2. There are financial incentives.

This is one of the main reasons why women (especially B-class females) stay with men who are blatant cheaters. Whenever a very attractive woman from Los Angeles asks me for my advice on dealing with a cheating mate, it's almost always the same scenario.

The woman will say something like "Tariq, I'm dating this guy, and we've been together for a year. He's married, but he and his wife have been separated for two years. He lives out of town, and I go see him once a month. Every time I call his house, different females answer the phone. And he has admitted to cheating on me at least one time. But he said that was it . . . What should I do?"

After they tell me something like this, the first thing I ask is "So, what team does he play for?" And almost every time, the female will say, "He plays for the Atlanta Falcons (or whatever team), but that's not why I'm with him."

The reality is, that's *exactly* why she's with him. Because when I see that a woman (especially an attractive female) is trying *that* hard to find a reason to justify being in a relationship that is blatantly dysfunctional, there is always a major piece of the puzzle missing. And in most cases, that missing piece of the puzzle is money.

In many cases, if a woman is in a relationship where she is receiving material and monetary kickbacks, or even if she thinks there is a possibility of financial gain in the future, she will be willing to endure all types of seemingly unacceptable behavior.

The reality is, when women are faced with the age-old dilemma of being a rich man's mistress or a poor man's wife, many women are willing to share the lap of luxury with other women. This is why it is important for women to start getting their own finances together at a young age, so they won't be confronted with this dilemma.

3. They feel they lack other options.

Many woman stay with men who are cheaters because they don't think that anyone else would want them. Some have such a need for attachment that they will stay in this type of relationship simply out of fear of being alone.

It's amazing that there are still women out there who think that a bullshitting man is better than no man. This is why it is important for women to become comfortable and confident with themselves. Confidence is something that no one else can give you. You have to give it to yourself.

4. They are embarrassed to let other people know that they have a failed relationship.

Women will stay with cheaters because they are more concerned with putting up the front of having the perfect relationship than having to accept reality, and moving on to a better situation.

Too many women define themselves based on their relationships. The relationship or marriage becomes their whole identity, and when the relationship fails, these women feel like they are losing their identity.

Ladies, when it comes to rectifying your relationships or your general well-being, stop worrying about what other people might say or what "they" think. You need to worry about what is best for you. Because at the end of the day, "they" are going to be concerned about "their" business—not yours.

5. They don't want the other woman to "win."

Many women have competitive natures. Often they will stay in a relationship with a cheating man simply to spite the other female, because these women don't want to have to live with the thought of another woman "taking" her man.

The reality is, a man can't be taken if he doesn't want to be took. He is not a hostage. You can't kidnap a dick. A cheater cheats because he wants to cheat, not because someone forces him. And blaming the other woman (or women) and taking your frustrations out on her (or them) is just another way of not dealing with the truth.

Should a woman forgive and forget or rise up and split?

When a woman finds out that her man has cheated on her, the fact that he had sex with another woman isn't as traumatizing as the fact that he has lied to her. Women like to feel comfortable in relationships, and it is impossible to feel a sense of comfort around a person you can't trust.

One common reason why men cheat is that they encounter no negative repercussions. People will do what you allow them to do. And if a man sees that you are the type of woman who will look the other way when he is doing his dirt, he will push the envelope as far as he can.

We've all seen those lie detector shows on daytime TV where the man was caught cheating, and the woman stayed with him anyway. These men have no problem with being dishonest, because they know they can get away with it. And if a woman is at the point where she has to give her man lie detector tests, send private investigators to follow him, or snoop through his things because she doesn't trust him, she should not be in a relationship with him.

Usually, when you *suspect* your mate is cheating on you, he is. If a man finds out his woman is cheating on him, he's out. Just like that. No explanation needed. No more words need to be said. The average man will not remotely tolerate being in a relationship with a cheating woman. But a woman can have concrete evidence that her man is cheating, and she will still stick around, and say things like "Before I leave him, I need to confront him with the evidence." Or "I need to bring *closure* to this situation." What she is really saying is "I'm going to give him an opportunity to tell me a better lie."

For a man to confess to cheating, he has to be caught in the act, red-handed. And the reasons these men give their women as to why they cheated are pretty typical. Sometimes men can get creative with their excuses, but for the most part, they all read from the Cheaters Handbook.

The top five excuses cheating men give their women:

1. "I was drunk, and one thing led to another."

2. "You and I were going through problems, and it was only that one time."

3. "Well, she *is* the mother of my kids," or "We have a history together."

4. "She reminded me of you."

5. "I have a sexual addiction . . . and I need help."
   (This is one of my personal favorites, because it's the one that Eric Benet told Halle Berry.)

When women try to use rationalizations like "He *owes* me the truth," and "I *deserve* to know if he's lying or not," they are simply not being realistic about how relationships work, and how life works.

In life *and* relationships, nobody owes you anything. And if you are in a relationship, and your mate is being dishonest, should he be more truthful? Yes. Should he be upfront about everything? Yes. But we don't live in a world of what *should* be. We live in a world that *is*. There should be no hunger or racism in the world, but there is. And people have to learn how to work around that.

In a relationship, there should be no infidelity. But unfortunately there often is. Your mate doesn't owe you the truth, you owe it to yourself to learn the truth. And if you are in a relationship, and you know your man is cheating, and you continue to allow him to tell you lie after lie and excuse after excuse, that's *your fault*. You owe it to yourself to deal with reality.

Tip #8 on how women can have game:

Don't rely on the "be-a-bitch" tactic to get quality men.

Many women feel if they are too nice or too submissive, guys will try to walk all over them. So many women try to adopt the "be-a-bitch" mentality as a defense mechanism. These women figure if they act like a bitch, guys are less likely to try to get over on them. First of all, if a man is scandalous, he's going to be scandalous whether you act like a bitch or not. Plus, the only men who would allow women to use "be-a-bitch" tactics on them are wimpy guys who are passive and submissive. And ladies, do you *really* want a guy like that?

9: Why Do Men Seem Afraid to Commit?

There is a very simple scenario going on in today's dating scene: Women want to get married . . . And men don't. And women want to know why.

Some of the most common reasons we hear are "Women in their thirties and forties are independent and they have their own careers, and they intimidate men," and "Men are afraid to open up their emotions to commit."

Let me speak for a majority of men out here, ladies. First of all, this notion of men being afraid and intimidated by independent, successful career women is bullshit. This is something that many women tell each other to justify their inability to get into lasting relationships.

Ladies, your independence and career are not intimidating or scary to men. It's not like your career is the Blair Witch. Men are not hiding in the woods, trembling in fear, talking about "I just met a woman who makes twenty dollars an hour, and *I am so scared.*" It's not that serious to us.

The problem is that successful career women in their thirties and forties have a tendency to bring that competitive work
ethic mentality into their relationships. And this creates a
power struggle.

Men are not intimidated by being in a power struggle with
a woman—we are just turned off by it. But if you are the kind
of woman who can leave her work mentality *at work,* men
won't have a problem with you.

When a man has been out working all day, and dealing
with the struggle of daily living (especially a black man,
because he has to go through that extra shit), the last thing he
wants to do is come home to a power struggle.

The only men that would be intimidated by a successful
female would be the scrub and parolee types. And if you are a
successful woman, would you really want those types of guys
anyway?

It's not the commitment that men fear. Men are afraid of
the *consequences* if the commitment doesn't work out.

As I stated before, with the way current laws and legal sys-
tems are set up today, men simply cannot afford to make a
commitment to the *wrong* female. Because back in the day, if a
man and woman were in a relationship, and it didn't work out,
they could just simply go their separate ways. No harm, no
foul. (I'm not talking about situations where men have families, then leave the wife and kids in financial turmoil. I'm talking about relationships where the two people left with what
they came in with.)

But today, if a man makes a commitment to the wrong
woman, he could end up financially ruined. So men aren't
afraid of commitment—they are afraid of the possibility of losing their house. They are afraid of getting their wages garnisheed. They are afraid of being indebted to someone else for

the rest of their lives. And men know that all this can happen just from *dating* someone. So marriage is really something that most men are not too gung-ho about.

The Real Deal on Marriage

What is the real meaning of marriage? Marriage is about two people who share a common bond—two people who want to join together as one and raise a family, and have each other's best interests at heart.

Well, that's the "brochure" explanation of what marriage is. This is the brochure that society uses to sell the marriage vacation. But we all know that often the brochure's description and the actual vacation are two totally different things. Have you ever seen a brochure for a luxury cruise vacation? It might say "Come take our cruise! You'll sail on a luxury liner, have four-star meals, and gamble at our twenty-four-hour casino." And when you get to the pier, you see that it's really a tugboat, with hot wings and a deck of Uno cards.

This is what marriage is like to men. See ladies, marriage means something totally different to men than it does for women. The myth that is perpetuated in society today is that more women than men are for the idea of marriage because women have a better capacity to love, have more compassion, and more dedication than men.

Well, we've all seen how vicious some women can get during divorce proceedings. All that love, compassion, and dedication is nowhere to be found then. So we all know that's not the real reason why so many women want to get married today.

Just look at the reality TV shows like *Who Wants to Marry*

a Millionaire and *Joe Millionaire.* When you have dozens of women willing to compete for the opportunity to marry a total stranger, you have to wonder if this is really about love, compassion, and dedication.

Love, compassion, and dedication are what marriage *used* to be about, but today, most women don't buy into the brochure definition of marriage. The reality is this: Women look at marriage as something that will save them. And men look at marriage as something that will destroy them.

Both men and women look at each other's view of marriage as being unrealistic and immature. Women think that men don't want to grow up and take responsibility. And men feel that women are simply intrigued with fulfilling their childhood dream of a fairy tale wedding.

Both of these perceptions have validity. There are many men who don't want to get married because they hope that once they get that record deal, that big promotion, or that NFL contract, they are gonna be bangin' hoochies left and right. And they don't want a marriage to get in the way of that.

And many women want to get married because they want to have a Prince Charming/Cinderella lifestyle, where the husband will "make everything all right."

In marriage, there are pros and cons. For women, there are more pros than cons. And the way many men look at marriage today, there are no pros for them—just cons. The cold hard truth is this, ladies—and I represent a *lot* of men out there. There are benefits for women in marriage. But in this day and age, men feel like there are really no benefits or reasons to get married. Let's look at some of the benefits on each side.

Benefits that a woman gets from marriage:

1. The ultimate form of attention—her wedding day.
   A day where all the attention is focused on her.
   A day that she has been dreaming about all her life.

2. Someone to help her pay the bills, and generally,
   the *majority* of the bills (not counting the few
   relationships where you have a Sugar Mama who
   pays all the bills in the marriage).

3. She gets to start a family before her biological
   clock stops ticking.

4. If the marriage breaks up, she gets to keep half
   the man's belongings, and he still supports her
   for years to come.

Those aren't bad benefits for women. Now let's look at how men view marriage.

"Benefits" that a man gets from marriage:

1. He has to give up dating other women.

2. He has to go to work and provide for another
   person.

3. If things don't work out, he gets to financially
   support the woman while she dates other people.

Ladies, are you really surprised that men aren't flocking to the altar, ready to sign up for this? Not only do men feel that the laws regarding marriage are stacked against them, thanks to the feminist movement, the *traditional* roles of marriage are even looked down upon in our society.

Since the 1960s, women have heard how marriage is oppressive and that women should not be reduced to doing housework and other domestic activities. So the average man really sees no incentives for him to get married.

This isn't to say that there aren't any guys out there who want to get married. If a man is in a relationship with a woman who sincerely has his best interest at heart, when the topic of marriage comes up, he would take that into serious consideration.

But many men feel that most women want to get married for selfish reasons that really have nothing to do with the man. Oftentimes, when women discuss marriage with men, men feel like the woman's motives are disingenuous. Women make the marriage all about *them,* and men feel like *their* best interest isn't being taken into consideration. All men hear are women saying "I," "my," and "me." Women will say things like:

"We need to get married because":

1. *"I* ain't getting no younger."

2. *"I* deserve *my* wedding day."

3. *"My* biological clock is ticking."

4. "All *my* friends are getting married."

5. *"My* mama keeps pestering *me* about getting married."

6. *"I* need a ring on *my* finger."

To men, this sounds less like a commitment, and more like a charity case. Because the nonverbal message in all of this is "I need help, and I don't care who gives it to me."

Men in this situation feel that the women are more in love with the *idea* of marriage than they are concerned with the men themselves. And in many cases, the real reason a lot of women want to get married is because they feel like they are beginning to run out of options.

Are there women who want to get married because they sincerely have a desire to satisfy and enhance the well-being of a specific person they are dating? Sure there are. But let's take a look at the real dialogue that women have with themselves when it comes to the issue of marriage:

"I'm twenty-nine . . . I've had my fun . . . I'm not getting any younger . . . I have a lot of credit card debt . . . I have a lot of student loan debts . . . My biological clock is ticking . . . I've been bullshitting around in relationships with all of these other no-good guys . . . I'm tired of getting up and going to work at this funky job every day . . . So I really *need* a husband."

The dialogue that men have with themselves is very different. It's more like:

"I'm twenty-ninee . . . I'm getting more play from better women as I get older . . . I don't have a biological clock, so I can have kids whenever I want . . . I'm about to be making more paper than I did before . . . I'm just now beginning to have my fun . . . So I don't need a wife right now."

Common Mistakes Women Make When Trying to Get a Man to Commit

Women make three basic mistakes when they are trying to get a man to commit to marriage.

1. They try to give the man an ultimatum.

2. They avoid accepting the truth.

3. They close off their options.

Ultimatums

Presenting a man with the "You better marry me or else" scenario hardly ever works, because men hate being forced to do something against their will. Even if they do agree to commit, they will be resentful toward you in the long run.

Plus ladies, you shouldn't even *want* to be in a relationship where you have to twist someone's arm until he gives in. What does that say about you?

Not Wanting to Accept the Truth

Women are more intrigued with the *journeys* in life. Men are intrigued with the *destinations* in life. And this pertains to almost every aspect of men's and women's lives. For example, when a man needs a certain article of clothing, say a jacket, he usually concerns himself with a destination. And that destination is the mall, where he buys the jacket and then goes back home.

Now let's say a woman needs a particular article of clothing, for instance, shoes. She is usually not just concerned with the destination of going to the mall, picking up some shoes, and coming back home. The trip to the mall becomes a *journey,* because now she wants to look at some skirts, look at some handbags, and look at some makeup.

This theory also affects how men and women look at television. We all know that men like to watch sports on TV. Men like sports, because at the end of the game, their team is going to reach a *destination.* Men know there is going to be a definitive winner, or a definitive loser. Point blank.

Women, on the other hand, like to watch soap opera–type shows, where there is no definitive ending or destination. Soap opera plots are like journeys, because their story lines go on and on, and continue for years.

This theory even applies to the sexual natures of men and women. When men are having sexual intercourse, they are generally concerned with one destination: an orgasm.

When women are engaged in intercourse, they are more intrigued by the foreplay and the *buildup to the orgasm* than the orgasm itself. Women can have sex and not even reach an orgasm, and they are fine with that. Women are more turned on by the *journey* of sex than the *destination* of the orgasm.

This theory also applies to the way men and women look at relationships. When men are on the dating scene, they want to reach a certain destination with the females they meet.

If a man is looking for a potential wife, he will date that woman and marry her. If a man is looking for a potential booty call *until* he finds his wife material, he will get that as well.

Now when women date guys for five or six years, then complain that these guys aren't being decisive about whether or not they want to get married, the reality is this: if a guy has been just *dating* you for five or six years—guess what? He *has* made a decision. He has decided that he's *not* going to marry you. And many women might not want to accept the truth, because they are content with the *journey* of the relationship.

Destinations keep you grounded in truth. But *journeys* give you the opportunity to fantasize and speculate about what the outcome will be.

Like I said before, all relationships are somewhat of a gamble. But in order to increase your possibility of winning, you have to place bets where the odds are in your favor.

Now a woman might be in a relationship with a man, and

based on everything he has said and done, there is a 95 percent chance that they are *not* going to get married. But the woman may still focus on that 5 percent *possibility,* because the man told her that he might think about it, just to get her off his back.

The problem in too many relationships is that the woman stays in the relationship, relying on this 5 percent possibility of marriage, despite all of the verbal *and* nonverbal messages to the contrary. Many women put their lives in a cliffhanger, soap opera scenario because they are more comfortable with the journey of fantasizing about the day he might come to his senses and pop the question, rather than facing the reality of the situation. Once you accept reality, you *have* to get out of the comfort zone of fantasy, and begin to take action and make changes.

Not Having Any Options

Another major mistake women make is letting the relationship become their total identity. Everyone wants to be identified with something that gives them validity. And when women haven't found anything else in life they feel they can identify themselves with, they will often try to identify themselves through relationships (this is why many women will use terms like "housewife," "homemaker," or "stay-at-home mom" when describing themselves).

In many cases, the relationship a woman is in becomes her whole *life* and identity. And if the relationship happens to end, the woman may feel that her life and identity are ending.

Notice when certain women's relationships have ended, you will often hear them say things like "I felt like my whole world came crashing down," or "I felt like my life was over."

This is why it is important for women always to have *options* in life and relationships. Which brings us to:

Play or Be Played Rule #8

Never let a relationship monopolize your whole identity.

When people know that they have a monopoly over you, they think they can treat you any way they want.

If you want to get your driver's license, there is only one place you can go—the DMV. The DMV has a monopoly on issuing driver's licenses to people. Whenever you go there, they treat you like shit. The lines are hella long. The employees are oftentimes rude, and they seem to take their sweet time assisting customers. And they do this because they know we can't go anywhere else to get our licenses. We just have to stand there and take it. The public has no other options, so the DMV workers have no incentive to treat the customers better.

This same theory also applies to relationships. When you are in a relationship with certain men, and they know that you want to get married because you are coming across as if you have no other options, they will treat you any way *they* want to treat you. Some guys might string you along. Some might lie. And some might even cheat. They will do whatever they damn well please, because they know that you have no other options and you aren't going anywhere anyway.

This is why it is important for women to have other options. And when I say options, I don't mean dick on the side. Too many dicks makes a woman crazy, and it creates too much baggage. Too many women make the mistake of choosing the dick on the side option when they are having problems with their men.

Ladies, when you get mad at your man, then go out and give up some revenge coochie with some other guy, not only does this *not* make you feel better, it also makes you a potential candidate for the *Maury Povich Show*. And having people run up in your cooch because you are mad at your man isn't punishing him; it's punishing *you*.

You need to have other options like a career, or other special interests to focus on to show your mate that you do have a life outside of the relationship. What's the best way to figure out which options to choose? You gotta get life experience.

Accumulating Life Experience

There is a big world out there. And ladies, you've got to get out there and peep it out. A lot of women don't know what they want to do in life, because they haven't been anywhere to see what the world has to offer.

This is why it is important for you to experience life and try new things. Now, this doesn't mean going out and trying new designer drugs. This doesn't mean having a threesome with a goat and a midget. This doesn't mean experimenting with bisexuality. I mean accumulating some proactive, positive experiences.

Play or Be Played Rule #9

Accumulating positive experiences leads to *options*, and accumulating negative experiences leads to *baggage*.

Ladies, you need to read different books on different subjects. Go to places you have never been. Travel to cities you have never seen. Get out of an environment that will limit you or enable nonproductive activity. Get out of your mama's house.

Cut some of those chickenhead homegirls you have loose. Stop being in an "on and off" relationship with the same guy you've been dating since you were fifteen.

Do whatever it takes to shake those old habits of immobility, and get out there and experience new and different things. When you become more worldly, you then have the ability to reference certain things.

We all have an interest in people we have things in common with. And when you can reference things that you and other people have in common, this is a great foundation for a friendship that has the potential to turn into a relationship.

For instance, if you are a female living in New York, and you just met a man who recently moved into town from Atlanta, you could share with him how you spent your last vacation in Atlanta. Or if you met a man who is a doctor, you can gain a rapport with him by sharing your insight from books you've read pertaining to medical issues. Or if you met a man who likes fine dining you can discuss your favorite upscale restaurants.

It's always good to try to know a little bit about everything. I'm shocked to see that there are many women who are in their late twenties and early thirties who have never been outside the state where they were born. If you haven't done anything, or been anywhere outside of your immediate hood, what could you possibly have in common with anyone, besides the people in your hood?

This is why you have to live a little. Try things. Treat life like a treasure hunt. Get out there and look under a few rocks, because you never know what you might uncover. You might find something that you are extremely passionate about. And when you have other passions you can focus on, you'll be less vulnerable to being monopolized by a relationship.

When you are in a relationship with a man, and he sees that you are focusing on other things that you are passionate about, he knows that if he doesn't act right, the *potential* of you possibly meeting and getting with somebody else is always a factor. So this gives him the incentive to give you better "customer service" in the relationship.

Tip #9 on how women can have game:

Always exercise self-control.

Getting drunk, getting high, having temper tantrums, giving up the ass too quick, overeating, and so on are usually signs of lack of self-control. Men like a woman with some form of discipline in her life. And no man with anything going for him wants to invest in a woman with loose, unstable behavior.

10: Successful Black Men Who Date Other Races— Myths and Reality

The question of why successful black men tend to date outside their race has been a very popular topic in the black community for years. And year after year, people have been coming up with the same tired, redundant, clichéd reasons for this phenomenon.

Most people (especially men) are afraid to address this topic correctly and honestly, because they fear the negative backlash they may receive from black women. But I want black women to win in the dating game. And I would be doing the sistas a disservice by letting these myths perpetuate.

The first myth that I would like to address is the myth that there is a shortage of available black men. When sistas buy into this myth, they also buy into the myth that white women take what few available black men are left.

The problem that sistas are *really* complaining about is not the shortage of available black men, but the shortage of available, *financially well off* black men.

Generally, women want a man with money. This is a fact of life. When men are growing up, they are taught to date the best looking woman they can get who is also sweet, loving, and charming, with good character. While women are growing up, they are taught to date a doctor or a lawyer. So a lot of women were basically taught to place a man's occupation over his character. And in some cases, substitute his occupation for his character.

There are rich, successful black men in many types of prestigious occupations. But for the sake of this topic, we are going to use professional black male athletes as the example. We all know that dating a professional athlete is like a badge of honor in female circles today (and because many women of every race are subject to the Cinderella mentality, pro athletes are the closest thing to Prince Charming for many women in the black community).

Professional athletes are the alpha males in our society today. They are young, tall, physically fit, and they are rich.

The desire of women to get with an athlete has gotten so intense that club promoters send out flyers with pictures of professional athletes on them. These promoters know that if they announce that a certain professional athlete is going to be at a club, women will flock there.

And if you go to the average nightclub in any major U.S. city, there could be a thousand normal, nine-to-five-type brothas there who have good character. But half the women in the club will be trying to cram into the VIP room to gather around the three professional athletes in the place.

And this is the complaint that brothas have. Black men who are not rich complain that they simply get passed over by many sistas. Females, especially attractive ones, simply can't get with the idea of dating a guy who isn't ballin'.

These sistas aren't concerned with the reasons why a brotha isn't ballin' outta control. They don't care that the average black man has had generations of obstacles, such as institutionalized racism, to deal with that have limited his potential to become a millionaire or baller.

We don't live in a world of "why," we live in a world that "is." And these women want a man who "is" financially rollin', *right now*. And there is nothing wrong with that. You can't knock people for liking what they like, and wanting what they want. My thing is, just be honest about what you want.

So many women are afraid of being labeled a gold digger or predator, that they go out of their way to sugarcoat their real desires. Ladies, if you want a baller, admit, to yourself, at least, that you want a baller. But you must understand that you should follow the proper procedures to get with a man of financial means.

And sistas, telling yourself you can't get a ballin' black man because all the white women are taking them isn't going to help you in the long run.

Myths and Realities

Let's take a look at some of the most common myths and clichés about rich black men who date white women:

Myth #1: White women are like trophies for black men who have gained success.

The Reality: A trophy is something that you can display as a way of gaining respect. If a white woman is a rich black man's trophy, who is he going to display his trophy to? A black man parading a white woman around other white people isn't going to get him any extra respect. And him parading his white woman around black circles will *definitely* not get him any extra respect. So we can eliminate this myth as the reason successful black men date white women.

Myth #2: Successful black men date outside their race because they know that white women will take more shit from them than a black woman would.

The Reality: This happens to be one of the more popular myths about this topic. It also happens to be the biggest crock of BS ever adopted by women on the dating scene.

The reality is, sistas take the *same shit* from a man that the white girls do, and more so. There are black women who are dating guys who work at Popeye's Chicken, and these brothas are coming home and cursing these sistas out every night.

There are sistas out there who are dating unemployed parolees who are sleeping with them, their cousins, and their best friends. And these women will *still* tolerate these guys. So we can eliminate the myth that white women are more prone to negative behavior from black men, because we all know that is not true.

Myth #3: Successful black men date white women because they can now afford to get the "forbidden fruit."

The Reality: The "forbidden fruit" myth may have had some validity in the late 1960s and early '70s, but this is a new millennium. And brothas today have had access to white women for a long time now. So there's nothing forbidden about that fruit.

Myth #4: Successful black men have been tricked into accepting blonde-haired white women as the ultimate standard of beauty.

The Reality: All of Western civilization has accepted blondes as the standard of beauty. Even *black women* have accepted blondes as the standard of beauty.

When little black girls are growing up, they are flooded with images and commercials for Barbie dolls. Even today, if you watch any television programs or channels geared at children, you will see Barbie commercials about every twenty minutes. And Barbie is one busy little chick. She has a dreamhouse, beach house, condo, Corvette, and a swimming pool. Barbie has a gang of stuff.

And many black females grew up seeing all this Barbie merchandise day in and day out. And then we wonder why we have some sistas out here walking around with a blonde weave. That's because many sistas have accepted the blonde standard of beauty. Look at some of the most famous young black females in the entertainment industry today. Many of them have gone the blonde route at some point or another. You see as many blondes on BET as you do on MTV. Here are a few examples:

- Eve
- T-Boz
- Lil' Kim
- Beyoncé
- Faith Evans
- Mary J. Blige
- Jada Pinkett
- Venus and Serena Williams

This list could go on and on.

And Latina women uphold this standard as well. Christina Aguilera has gotten her blonde on. And J-Lo has been known to throw in her blonde highlights on occasion.

So the rationale for a lot of successful brothas is, "Since so many different females are trying to be bleached blondes, and since I have the means to attract any type of woman I want, I might as well get the real thing."

Myth #5: Black men hate themselves; that's why when they get money, they go date white women in order to try and escape their blackness.

The Reality: Ladies, I want you to really feel me on this one . . . Peep the real . . . No one loves themselves more than a rich American black man. Rich black men are almost arrogant with the love they have for themselves. American black men are the most loved and hated people in the world. If a black man is broke, he is looked upon as the scum of the earth. When a black man is rich, he is praised throughout the world. (Until he gets caught up in a scandal. Then he is thrown in with the rest of the broke brothas.)

The American black man has a style and flavor that is emulated by other cultures around the world. If you go to countries such as Japan and England you will see people trying to adopt the style of the American black man.

Even white men who *act* like black men become the shit. Look at Elvis. Here's a white guy who got on stage and basically did an *impression* of black entertainers like Little Richard and Chuck Berry. And he became the king of rock and roll. Even today, who is the biggest hip-hop artist in the world? That's right, Eminem. And all he does is emulate what he saw growing up in a black community.

Rich American black men have more options than rich celebrities of any other race. When a celebrity like Sylvester Stallone walks into a club, he will mostly attract white women. When Ricky Martin or Enrique Iglesias walks into a spot, they might get more play from Latina females. But when a black NBA player comes into a club, every race and nationality in the crayon box starts sweating these guys.

So not only do rich black men love themselves, they have more options to kick it with all the other races of women who are feeling them as well.

Myth #6: Rich black men like white women because white women do freaky things that black women wouldn't do.

The Reality: Now sistas, we *all* know that this is BS. There are black women who will lick, suck, and eat the same things that the white girls will. The difference between white girls and black girls is a lot of white girls will do freaky shit to almost anyone they date.

But many black women have a VIP list for doing freaky shit. Now, a sista might not perform oral sex on a guy who works at Wal-Mart. But let it be a guy who makes $10 or $15 million and that sista will break her neck suckin' that dick. So we can really eliminate that myth.

Since we have debunked all of the myths, what's the real deal? Why is it that so many successful black men end up with white women? One of the real reasons is financial compatibility.

Financial and Social Compatibility

Most young, financially well-off men such as professional athletes want to date women who were down with them before they made money, or they want to date young, financially well-off women. This has nothing to do with race. Due to circumstances in our society, there just happen to be more young, financially well-off white women in this country than well-off women of other races. Often, white women have received secondary gains from their families, putting them in a better financial position.

Another stereotype is that these rich black men are going out and "saving" white trailer trash women. This is a myth that has been put out to make women of other races feel better.

I have personally seen interactions with ballers and their white wives and girlfriends, and many of these women are from places like Beverly Hills and other affluent neighborhoods around the country. And again, this isn't about race. Because if a young, attractive black woman has the same type of money that the ballers have, she has no problem getting a professional athlete or any other type of financially stable man. Just look at Tyra Banks, Holly Robinson, or Gabrielle Union.

The list could go on and on. The point is, all these sistas have or are dating a professional athlete, and they have dated other types of financially stable men. Why? Because these women were financially and socially compatible with the men they dated.

Play or Be Played Rule #10

The people you date will usually
be a reflection of you, and where
you are mentally and socially.

When you are dating someone, that person is either going to be an asset to the relationship or a liability. Either they are going to bring something to the table, or they are going to take something off the table.

Money *does* change people. Men and women act differently and carry themselves differently when they have money (some people start acting different when they get their paychecks on Fridays). And a black man with paper has more in common with a black woman with paper.

Now a rich white man can afford to date or marry a woman who is a liability. A lot of white men can afford to lose a few million bucks, because they know there's more money where that came from. But a rich black man is a different story.

First of all, for a black man to become a millionaire, he had to beat every odd and obstacle that this country has set up for brothas. So when a brotha is sitting on a few million bucks, he knows that if he brings the wrong people around him, he might end up back in the 'hood with no dough.

That's why financially stable brothas like dealing with women who are familiar with at least being *around* money. A lot of women like a financially stable man because of the material things he has. A lot of women don't care how the guy got the material items. They just like the fact that he has them.

Now a lot of financially stable guys like females who have material things as well. But these guys are more impressed by the knowledge and expertise the woman used in order to achieve those material items than the material items themselves.

And when you see a young, attractive black woman with nice financial credentials, that means she really had game to get hers. There aren't too many black folks getting inheritances or trust funds. So if a brotha had to hustle for his paper, if he gets with a sista, most likely she had to hustle for hers.

And the reality is, in this country, there are a lot of young white women who don't have to hustle as hard for their paper. And these women get their pick of financially stable men—including brothas.

Now I've heard a lot of people say things like "Rich brothas should be more sympathetic as to *why* many young black women don't have the kind of financial background that young white women have." Like I said in the beginning of this chapter, we don't live in a world of "why," we live in a world that "is."

People rarely date out of sympathy. Just like many attractive women aren't sympathetic to the plight of the regular nine-to-five brothas who aren't making a lot of money, many rich brothas aren't sympathetic toward the plight of the nine-to-five sistas who aren't making major paper either.

What Many Ballin' Brothas Look for in Women (White or Black)

Rich brothas look for women who are assets to the relationship. Women may assume that since a brotha is already rich, he couldn't possibly need anything from the woman. But a rich brotha wants a female who has had some financial stability in her life, so she can at least come to the table with some *ideas* on maintaining finances.

If a ballin' brotha is going through some financial difficulties, he wants to be able to turn to his significant other for some input on how to rectify the situation. Now, if he is in a relationship with a sista who had her finances in order when she met him, she could turn him on to some lucrative business opportunities that have worked for her in the past.

If the rich brotha is in a relationship with a white woman

who comes from a family with money, even if *she* doesn't have any financial expertise, she can at least give him the names of some financial experts, lawyers, or stockbrokers that have dealt with her family.

Now, if the same rich brotha is in a relationship with a hoodrat or a trailer chick, and he is going through some financial difficulties, how can this type of female be of assistance in the situation? Besides maybe knowing a few drug dealers, these women don't have any useful connections. And these rich brothas know that when the money is gone, this type of female is gone. Which brings up another very important topic regarding rich black men.

Scam Artists

I don't want you to think that just because many ballers and athletes get with white women, this means that white women are on a higher moral plateau than sistas. There are plenty of white women who are just as scandalous as women of any other race. And white women pull scams on rich men (black and white) all the time. Black women pull scams on men as well; the only difference is, white female scam artists are better at it than black female scam artists.

In our social subculture, you have:

- white hustlers—and white scam artists
- black hustlers—and black scam artists

Black hustlers are usually more thorough than white hustlers. But white scam artists are generally better scammers than black scam artists. White scam artists usually think out their scams before they execute them. Black scam artists have the "smash and grab" mentality.

For instance, a sixteen-year-old black male scam artist and a sixteen-year-old white male scam artist may get totally different results from their scams. The sixteen-year-old black male might do something like rob a liquor store at gunpoint, steal $60, get caught, and end up getting twenty-five years to life.

Whereas the sixteen-year-old white guy will get on the Internet, learn how to crack secret security codes, and *embezzle* $600,000. And if he gets caught, he just has to play dumb, and he will most likely get away with it.

Black and white female scam artists are no different. If either one of these types of women were planning to scam, say, a black male professional athlete or any other type of rich man, they would go about it in two different ways.

A white female scam artist will play the supersubmissive, Goody two-shoes role, until she *really* gets her foot in the door. A white female scam artist will at least wait until her name is on some paperwork before she drops the ball, and shows her true colors.

White female scam artists don't scam for peanuts. They scam for the big chips. So when they drop the bomb on a guy, they are gonna get him for at least half of what he has.

Whereas the black female scam artist has one little scam up her sleeve—the pregnancy hustle. When a black female scam artist gets around a professional athlete, the first thing she is going to do is try to get pregnant.

The Trap-a-Baller Scam

Many rich brothas, like pro athletes, are reluctant to have serious relationships with women who are not in a stable financial position because of the many female "trap-a-baller" scam artists that are lurking in their midst.

The trap-a-baller scam is an advanced version of the pregnancy hustle. The only difference is, the pregnancy hustle is usually played by F-class females, and the trap-a-baller scam is usually played by B-class females.

B-class females (attractive women with no game) have the looks to at least gain access to professional athletes and other ballers. And what these B-class females do is try to sleep with as many athletes as they can, with the hopes of getting pregnant by one of them and living off the child support money.

This is a very common phenomenon among black professional athletes. So when these athletes are looking to date sistas who really have it together, they have the added challenge of having to weed out the trap-a-baller scammers. And there are more black females pulling this scam on black athletes than white women.

This isn't to say that there are any fewer white female scammers. I'm just saying that there are more black females who are trying to pull the pregnancy scam on black athletes.

See, this is still America. And the average white woman isn't really trying to bring an illegitimate *black* baby back into the white community (no matter how rich or famous the baby's father is). This will not go over well in the *poor* white community, and it definitely won't go over well in the *affluent* white community.

When a white woman (especially one from an upper-class white community) is dating one of these black pro athletes, she generally shows more dedication to these men. Because a white woman usually has to sacrifice more things and privileges in order to date a black man. In some cases, she has to risk being disowned by her family, and risk being labeled an outcast by her own community.

So the last thing that many of these white women are trying to do is hustle a baby out of these black athletes. But in the black community at large, not only is having children out of wedlock a common occurrence, it's actually *encouraged*. (The only place in the white community where the pregnancy hustle is not really looked down upon is in the poor white trash sector of that community).

A recent incident illustrates the consequences of what can happen to white women who try to pull the trap-a-baller hustle on black male athletes. This is the case of Michael Jordan and Karla Knafel.

Karla Knafel, a white woman, had an affair with Jordan around the early 1990s. When she became pregnant she told Jordan he was the father. Jordan eventually gave her $500,000 to keep hush-hush about the affair.

It turned out that the real father of the child was another black man who happened to be a professional baseball player (but he wasn't raking in any major dough). And Knafel has *another* kid by another black NBA player, Dale Davis.

Rumor has it that she doesn't have close ties to her family in Indiana (a white woman with *two* illegitimate black children, I can imagine she wouldn't), and she spends her time bouncing back and forth between different athletes.

Since Knafel is now in her forties, she can't pull the same trap-a-baller tricks on athletes anymore. And because of legal fees and other expenses, she probably has run out of the other money she has scammed. With two black children out of wedlock, she is probably an outcast in every community she goes to, so now she is desperate. She got so desperate, in fact, that she tried to step back to Michael Jordan and swindle him out of some more money.

She tried to extort an additional $5 million by filing a lawsuit against Jordan, claiming he promised her the money ten years earlier. Obviously, she thought the threat of going public with this lawsuit about their previous affair would make Jordan cough up some more dough.

But Jordan threw a wrench in her game by going public about the affair *himself*. And now Knafel is pretty much ass-out. She played her trump card, and lost. And now she is *really* going to be a social outcast. This just shows that when a white woman tries to pull the pregnancy hustle on a ballin' brotha, she has to go to the extreme, and pull out every trick she has up her sleeve. Either that white woman is going to come up big time, or she's going to fall on her face big time.

Many white women aren't willing to take that risk. So if a white woman is going to run a con game on a black man, she is going to try a different angle.

Why Rich Brothas Have to Be So Cautious

Many ballin' brothas would love to date women who have a genuine and sincere character, and they would like to be able to trust more people. But the reality is, rich guys—especially young, rich black men—are targets. Unfortunately, the main people a rich black man has to watch out for are people from his own community.

When a black rapper or a black athlete becomes successful, the majority of people from his community will applaud his success. But for every ten black men who give him his props, there are five other black men who are planning to rob him the first chance they get.

Whenever you see TV programs showing successful rappers or athletes going back to visit their old neighborhoods, you notice that these guys are usually wearing bulletproof vests, have an arsenal of guns, and are flanked by dozens of armed bodyguards. They have to do this to go to *their own neighborhoods where they grew up.* (I have yet to see any white entertainers go through this process while visiting their old neighborhoods.) So you can imagine how cautious successful brothas have to be around brothas they don't know.

And for every ten black women that give a successful black man props, there are five sistas that will try to scam him. This is the reality that a lot of successful black men have to deal with. This is why these guys can't judge people based strictly on race. They have to look at a person's general character, and the results of their character.

So these men won't date a white woman simply because she's white. And they won't date a black woman simply because she's black. They want to date the woman who has the best character.

And because it is so easy to file frivolous lawsuits nowadays, these guys have to be extra careful who they have around them. The average black male pro athlete can't even go on a date with a woman these days without the female having a press conference the next day, claiming he fondled her tittie, and how she wants a million bucks.

The problem with women trying to get pregnant by athletes has gotten so bad that the NFL has something called the Rookie

Symposium, where speakers come in and advise the new players on how to handle being in the league, and how to deal with the influx of women while they are on the road. These guys are warned to use their own condoms, because there are several cases of women poking holes in condoms. And they are also warned to flush used condoms down the toilet, because there are women who will actually take the used condoms out of garbage cans and try to impregnate themselves.

Some rookie symposiums include former hoochies and wannabe gold diggers who give their own testimonials warning the athletes about women like them. These women talk about trying to trap pro ball players by getting pregnant, trying to file frivolous lawsuits, and basically trying to get at their money any way they can. So you can see why these guys have to be cautious when it comes to dating.

The Difference Between Groupies, Gold Diggers, and Scam Artists

See the dating scene through the eyes of the ballers. These guys have to accept that there are many predatory types of women that they have to look out for. The three most common ones are *groupies, gold diggers,* and *scam artists.*

If you are in one of these categories, it's very important that you acknowledge to yourself that you are. This way, you can better understand what your true agenda is when dealing with a baller.

Like I said before, a scam artist is the type of female who wants to try to make a quick buck off an athlete or a baller. She will try to file frivolous lawsuits, and/or she will try to get pregnant.

Now a groupie is a female who is basically living in fantasy-land. She is the kind of female who has never grown out of the Cinderella story, and she is hanging around hoping that a pro athlete is eventually going to save her. And the thing about groupies is that they really don't *know* they are groupies. They think that they are actually friends of the athletes and other celebrities.

Many groupies will try to justify their behavior by stating things like "I know the last ten guys I dated were professional basketball players, but it's not like I *try* to talk to athletes . . . They all approach *me*." And the reason athletes "just happen" to approach them is because these females are always hanging out in places like the back door of the Staples Center, wearing catsuits.

These women carefully position themselves in places they know athletes frequent. Many people erroneously label some groupies as gold diggers. Groupies are women who hang around celebrities because it makes them feel important. A gold digger is a female hustler with a certain agenda.

A gold digger knows if a guy is just interested in sex with her. And she makes it her job to get as much as she can out of the guy before she has sex (*if* she has sex) with him. A baller will have sex with a groupie, then drop her back off in the 'hood. And all that groupie will be left with are memories and hopes. I actually have more respect for a true gold digger because at least she is going to get something out of the deal.

A real gold digger knows it takes money to make money. So she is smooth with her hustle. She looks and acts like money. Therefore, she will attract more money.

Some groupies and chickenheads *try* to look like money, but it doesn't really work. A groupie or chickenhead might boost a Donna Karan or Chanel outfit from the mall. But it still won't look right on her, if her *actions* give off the impression of poverty and broke-ness.

A real gold digger knows how to carry herself when she is around different people. She knows how to blend in around money. Everything a groupie does is to impress her friends. Her whole being is based on how other people will perceive her. She thinks that if she is connected to celebrities, this will somehow help her gain popularity among her hoochie circles.

A real gold digger couldn't care less about what the next female thinks about her. As a matter of fact, a real gold digger will rarely hang around with other women anyway. She is more focused on her game.

Many groupies often have someone that enables their groupie fantasy. These women often still live at home with their mothers or they live with a number of other groupies as roommates. This gives them a lot of idle time to fantasize about Prince Charming.

Whereas the gold digger has responsibilities, and she doesn't have time to sell herself fantasies. She has rent to pay. She has car notes to pay. Her time is valuable, and she knows that hanging out with celebrities and not getting anything out of it will cause her to *lose* money.

A groupie will get around a celebrity and eventually start begging for things. Begging for food. Begging for trips to the salon. Begging for drinks. Begging for things at the mall. The minute a female begs for anything, a baller automatically puts her into the groupie, chickenhead, or hoodrat category. All the respect for her goes out the door.

But a real gold digger wouldn't be caught begging if her life depended on it. Her game is tighter than that. One common technique that many real gold diggers use is to spend money on the ballers *first*. A lot of women who aren't hip to the game don't understand this tactic.

See, the gold digger knows that ballers are used to begging women, and females who run their mouths bragging about their *potential*. And the gold digger knows that these ballers are already going to have their defenses up when they deal with new women. So the gold digger will cause the baller to lower his defenses, by offering to take *him* on an expensive date. When a baller sees that a female is willing to bring something to the table for a change, this makes her stand out. With his defenses lowered, he feels more comfortable around her and he is more willing to do something for her in return.

The gold diggers' philosophy is, "If I'm gonna be in the game, I'm gonna be in it to win it. And I don't knock any real hustler's hustle."

Tip #10 on how women can have game:

Don't hate on the next female who is successful at doing her thing.

There is an old saying: "There is no explanation needed for success, and there are no excuses needed for failure." If you know of another woman who is successful, don't try to tear her down to make yourself feel better. If anything, you should observe and learn what her strategies were that made her successful. Then take notes. If she became successful in business, find out who some of her business contacts were. If she became successful as an actress, try to find out what agents and acting school she went to. Even if a woman became successful by doing something scandalous, you can still take notes and get some constructive information from that. If the woman became successful by sleeping with an old, rich man, find out if that old man has a brother or an old rich cousin that *you* can get with. Just don't knock the next girl's hustle. Because when you spend a lot of energy hating on someone, oftentimes this means you secretly desire what they have.

11: How to Become a Queen

Being a queen is not as hard as you might think it is. As a matter of fact, becoming a queen is more about what you *don't* do than what you have to do. You see, men and women start off differently in life. Men start off in life rough around the edges. Men have to work toward perfection and king status over a period of time.

Men have to go through many trials and tribulations before they can reach king status, because how a man becomes a king depends on how he achieved his knowledge and how he handled his different life experiences.

Women, on the other hand, have it much easier. Women start off in life almost perfect. Women start off as queens. And all a woman has to do is maintain her queenly-ness. Innocence in women has always been valued by societies. A woman who is untainted, so to speak, has always been most desired by men.

Now being innocent and untainted doesn't mean being

flawless or free of mistakes. Everyone makes mistakes, and everyone is going to continue to make mistakes at some point in their lives. But what makes a woman maintain her queenly- ness is how she acknowledges and handles the mistakes she makes.

Oftentimes, a women who makes mistakes and bad judg- ments will stick with those bad judgments just to save face. Wallowing in mistakes is what will downgrade a woman from her status as queen. Because continuing to make bad judg- ments creates baggage. And queens don't carry baggage. Whatever happens in a queen's life, she will always rise again to her elevated throne. And you can't rise to the top when you have baggage holding you down.

Many religions hold that if one confesses his sins or wrongdoings, he is immediately forgiven for them. I believe this ideology has practical uses as well. When you admit your mistakes, or at least acknowledge them to yourself, your sub- conscious mind automatically looks for ways to rectify those mistakes.

How Queens Handle Adversity

In many cases, when a woman makes a mistake in life, or faces some adversity, she will identify herself through those mis- takes. A woman might date a man who isn't right for her. Instead of admitting to herself that she simply needs to make better choices in men, she will perpetuate her mistake by telling herself that she isn't worthy of better men (or she might spout those old clichés about "all the good men are in jail, unemployed, gay, blah, blah, blah"). Many women have this "throw in the towel" mentality when they face certain little difficulties. If you want to maintain your queenly-ness, you can't throw in the towel every time something doesn't go your way, because part of maintaining your queenly-ness is how you maintain your dignity in times of adversity. And maintaining your status as a queen throughout life's difficulties will oftentimes steer you in the direction of success.

Recently, some friends and I went to a local Karaoke bar in Hollywood. Some of the guys who were with me were A & R reps from a major record label. Many A & R reps are known to frequent spots where there is raw talent just in case they run across someone with potential to become a recording artist.

The whole vibe of the place was festive and upbeat, and there were dozens of people going up on stage to perform. Among them were two young ladies who were going to sing an old song by SWV. Now throughout the night, there were a few technical difficulties—the volume on the stage mics would fade in and out a little. Nothing major. You could still hear the performers just fine.

When the two young ladies were onstage, you could see one complaining to her friend that her mic was not as loud as it should be. The friend had a look on her face like "go ahead and start singing anyway." But the complaining female just copped this throw-in-the-towel attitude. Because her microphone's volume was fading slightly in and out (you could barely tell that there was a problem at all) she had an attitude like "I'm gonna just walk through the words to this song and not even try to be good or entertaining, because things aren't going exactly as planned."

So she just stood there rolling her eyes, with her hands on her hips, looking bored, while she half-ass sang through the words of the song. Needless to say, this was beginning to bring the energy of the audience down. Now when it was the other girl's turn to sing, she stepped up to the forefront, and she ripped it. She didn't let any minor technical difficulties stop her from doing her thing. She just decided to sing louder. And the audience was loving her. She knew how to maintain her queenly-ness. When you are faced with adversity, you are going to do one of two things. You are going to step up, or you are going to punk out. The first girl who sang decided to punk out. The second girl decided to step up her game in the face of adversity. She showed that she was professional enough to overcome the kind of minor setback that happens from time to time when you are performing live. And her queenly, professional attitude impressed the A & R people I was with. They approached her (and not the other female she was with) and exchanged information with her. And they are currently working in the studio with this young lady.

When you carry yourself as a queen at all times, you will always be prepared when a lucrative opportunity presents itself.

Tips on Maintaining Your Status as a Queen

• Educate Yourself

No matter how good you look, you still need game and education to back up those looks. A man who has himself together likes to have a woman who can thoroughly represent him and their relationship as a unit when he needs her to.

• Command Respect

Madonna used to act scandalously to attract attention, and then wonder and whine about how men were always leaving her to marry and have babies with other women. She didn't act like a queen, so she couldn't keep a king. Notice that she became

Mrs. Guy Ritchie only after she calmed down and started dressing and acting respectably.

• Pay Your Bills

If you don't live with your man, pay your own bills and don't expect him to contribute. If he offers, cool, but make it clear you don't *need* the help. If you live with your man, pay your part. If you don't, you're giving the impression (1) that you can't afford to, or (2) that you don't care to. Neither of which is queenly behavior.

• Feed Your Man

You know why people say the way to a man's heart is through his stomach? Because it's true. If you can cook, figure out what his favorite meals are and make them. If you can't cook, then make sure your crib is well supplied with his favorite snacks and beverages.

• Find a Man Who Can Elevate You

A king is by definition a successful person. Avail yourself of his wisdom as you pursue your goals. Men like the opportunity to demonstrate their skills and knowledge; and you involve and interest him in the parts of your life that can only underscore your value to him. This is why it is important for you to choose a man who has worthwhile advice to give.

• Make Yourself an Asset

Show your king that you can be an asset to his career and/or financial health. Sharon Osbourne is a classic example of a D-class Female who elevated herself to queen status because of her business skills. While hoochies no doubt sweated Ozzy back in the day (and who knows, perhaps still do to this day),

Sharon remains the undisputed queen of the Osbourne empire, because she was instrumental in building it.

• Keep Your Word

Women can be emotional creatures, but queens rise above their moods. They say what they mean, and mean what they say, and therefore have integrity. Martha Stewart used to have game, but lost it by flouting instead of finessing the law. If she lied to her investors, colleagues, and employees, how do you think she is going to treat her man?

• Support Your Man

In relationships, you will inevitably have disagreements. How you handle them will determine whether or not the relationship will last. Always save face and make your man feel you've got his back, or he will wonder about you, and rightfully so.

• Embrace Your Man's Family and Friends (Including His Exes)

If a man introduces you to his family and friends, he perceives you as girlfriend material and not just a sex partner. Show that you deserve this treatment. Don't display jealousy over an ex. If their friendship survived the breakup, then it will survive you, and you need to accept that. Jada Pinkett Smith smoothly took on the role of Will Smith's queen by insisting on behaving as a mother, and not a stepmother, to his children from a previous marriage. Plus, Jada has stated that she has a very good relationship with Will's ex-wife. Now that's a real queen for you.

• Maintain a Network of Positive People

It is very important to hang around people who are doing big thangs or people who are at least trying to better themselves.

Constructive energy is very contagious. And when you feed off of other people's positivity, others will want to feed off yours.

• Find Something You Are Passionate About

This is one of the most important tips on how to maintain your status as a queen. It's very important to find some type of hobby (or hobbies) that you really like to do, no matter how insignificant it may seem to others. Because once you realize that you have the capacity to be passionate about one activity, you will be able to transfer that passion into other areas of your life. Many nonpassionate people are quick to criticize the success of celebrities such as Jennifer Lopez, calling her enormous success overhyped because her singing and acting skills are sub-par. Sure there are many artists who can sing and act better than Jennifer, but she has one passion that not too many other female entertainers can come close to fading. J-Lo can dance her ass off. Jennifer utilized the passion she had that made her an excellent dancer, and transferred that passion into her singing and acting career. And this is why she is so successful.

• Be Tactful

Remember, there is a time and place for everything. A queen knows that certain things may not be appropriate at all times. Tactfulness must be applied to your attitude, your style of dress, as well as your choice of words. A queen knows not to curse out a waiter in an expensive restaurant because they don't serve Aliza`e. A queen knows not to go to the mall in house shoes and hair rollers. A queen knows not to go to a funeral wearing a red catsuit. There is nothing wrong with keeping it real, but keeping it real doesn't mean keeping it rude. As a queen, you must always carry yourself like a lady. (Yes, there are some guys who still like that in a woman.)

• Get Your Workout On

Men who are kings are impressed by women who have the discipline to exercise and take care of themselves. Consistently working out shows mental strength as well. Also, when you work out, you feel better about yourself.

• Be Comfortable with Yourself

When it comes to accentuating your looks, remember, less is more. Kings are more impressed by women who simply highlight their features, instead of creating new features. Sure, there are guys who will want to have the occasional romp in the hay with the females who look all hoochified. But these men will often settle down with the females who look more normal. If you look in the newlywed section of *Jet Magazine* every week, notice you rarely see the women with the purple weaves and twenty tattoos getting married. You usually see the more natural looking women walking down the aisle.

• Always Rely on Your Game, and Not Your Coochie

Nowadays, too many women are taught that their coochie is gold. And this causes many women to rely solely on their coochies to get them over in life. In our society, the moment that a woman becomes sexually active, she realizes that her coochie has value to certain men. So automatically, many women try to figure out how to benefit from the value of their coochies. Many women also feel a great sense of power knowing that they can manipulate and control men who desire their coochies. What women need to understand is that coochie is equivelent to currency, but it is not gold. As a matter of fact, in ancient times, women were literally used as currency (some guys would make deals like trading four of their wives for two goats, etc.).

Now let's look at how paper currency is valued. A $20 bill is really just a simple piece of paper. The only thing that gives that piece of paper value is the gold standard that backs it. Now a $20 bill in Cuban money may be worth $1 in America, because Cuban currency is backed by a lower standard.

If you are a female who only has her coochie to bring to the table, and nothing else to back it up, you will have a lot of value where the standards are lower. You will have value in the 'hood. You will have value in the trailer parks. You will have value in the projects. But if you come around men whose standards are higher when it comes to women, you need something to back up that coochie. This is why you need game. Because your game is gold. The game you have is going to be the gold standard that will back you up in everything you do in life. And if you apply all the principles and strategies of this book to your everyday life, you are guaranteed to win.

Conclusion

Now let's recap all ten of the Play or Be Played Rules

1. A man does not have to like you to have sex with you.

2. A female's ability to attract attention will *get* a man, but what a woman does to receive appreciation will *keep* a man.

3. When a man's nonverbal language tells you what he's about, you'd better accept it.

4. The way you start off in a relationship is the way you will end up in a relationship.

5. If a man agrees with everything you say, no matter how far-fetched or unusual it is, he just wants to have sex with you.

6. All men love hoes—just not as girlfriends or wives.

7. When a man cheats, 80 percent of the time it has nothing to do with *you*.

8. Never let a relationship monopolize your whole identity.

9. Accumulating positive experiences leads to *options,* and accumulating negative experiences leads to *baggage.*

10. The people you date will usually be a reflection of you, and where you are mentally and socially.

Ladies, if you apply these ten simple rules to your interactions with men, your dating life will definitely run much smoother. And you must also remember that the most important element of the game is to be *comfortable* with yourself.

Whenever you are insecure about something, it will show in your game. Because you will be afraid that others will see the things that you are insecure about. Fortunately, most things that many women are insecure about can be changed at their own discretion. You have complete power to rectify your insecurities and uplift your self-image (that's why it's called *self*-image).

If you are insecure about people thinking you have a limited vocabulary, read more books. If you are insecure about people finding out you dance at a strip club, get another job or get with other people who are accepting of your line of work (like pimps).

If you are insecure about wearing clothes that expose your gut, go to the gym. If you are insecure about not having cute toes, wear some footies when you make love. If you are insecure about your thighs being too big, put down the cakes and pies. If you are insecure about what a man might think if he sees you without your weave, work on growing your real hair, and rocking a weave-less do.

If you have to park three miles away from the club because you are insecure about people seeing you in your bucket, work on saving your paper so you can get a better car. Don't try to work around or pacify your insecurities. You should always try to *rectify* your insecurities.

You can change or fix anything about yourself that you are insecure about. You don't always have to be 100 percent satisfied with yourself, because there should always be incentives in your life for growth. But you can *always* be comfortable with yourself.

Being comfortable with who you are gives you confidence. And the only way to always be comfortable and confident with yourself is knowing you have the game to achieve any goal you wish to achieve.

It doesn't matter how much makeup a woman wears, because makeup comes off. It doesn't matter how many fly clothes a woman has, because clothes go out of style. It doesn't matter how many expensive shoes a woman owns, because shoes wear out. It doesn't matter how much weave a woman puts in her hair, because weaves get matted up.

All these external items will come and go. But the thing that cannot be taken away from a person is *confidence.* And confidence is always the sexiest asset a woman has.

Ladies, whenever you are in the mood or a situation where you feel you need a little reinforcement in your game, you can always flip back to this handy list of key tips from *Play or Be Played.* You can Xerox some of these tips as well as the list of Rules on p. 201–2, and put them up on the fridge, post them at work, put them in your car, read them on the treadmill,

stick 'em in the bathroom, read them at the weave shop, post
them on your computer, send them to your homegirl who's in
jail for boosting, etc.

Tip #1   Always take full responsibility for your
            actions and decisions.

Tip #2   Try to smile as much as you can.

Tip #3   Become a "nonverbal language" reader.

Tip #4   Realize that in most cases, you can
            control your looks.

Tip #5   Learn to realize and accept when
            something isn't working for you.

Tip #6   Be comfortable in knowing that you
            have the power to accumulate the
            knowledge and game you need to
            improve yourself.

Tip #7   Respect the laws of physics.

Tip #8   Don't rely on the "be-a-bitch" tactic
            to get quality men.

Tip #9   Always exercise self-control.

Tip #10   Don't hate on the next female who
            is successful at doing her thing.

Notes

1. This ideology was confirmed through the literature of feminists like Ara Wilson of Ohio State University, and by popular feminist propaganda in the early '70s such as "Lesbians in Revolt" by Charlotte Bunch. *The Ferries: Lesbian/Feminist Monthly* (January 1972): 1 8–9.

2. Source: U.S. Department of Justice. U.S. Department of Health and Human Services.

3. Source: Planned Parenthood Federation of America.

4. Source: Population Action International.

5. Seventy percent of juveniles in jail, and 85 percent of men in prison grew up fatherless. Kids without fathers are ten times more likely to abuse drugs, etc. Source: U.S. Department of Health and Human Services. U.S. Department of Justice.

6. The children have poorer health, reduced educational attainments, and higher rates of behavior problems, and they are more likely to become adolescent parents themselves. Source: Population Resource Center.

7. Source: U.S. Department of Education.

8. *Time* magazine article entitled "Making Money Off Deadbeat Dads," September 2, 2002, reported that Support Kids, one of the biggest child support agencies, has collected more than $120 million, but they kept $40 million for themselves.

To inquire about Tariq's coaching services,
or to invite him to speak for your organization,
please contact:

Tariqn77@aol.com

Or go to
www.kingflex.org